God makes the rivers to flow.
They tire not, nor do they
cease from flowing.

God Makes

the Rivers to Flow

Selections from the
sacred literature of the world
chosen for daily meditation by

EKNATH
EASWARAN

NILGIRI PRESS

©1982, 1991 by the Blue Mountain Center of Meditation
All rights reserved. Printed in the United States of America
ISBN: cloth, 0–915132–69–9; paper, 0–915132–68–0

Second edition, first printing November 1991
The Blue Mountain Center of Meditation, founded in Berkeley in
1961 by Eknath Easwaran, publishes books on how to lead the
spiritual life in the home and the community.

For information please write to
Nilgiri Press, Box 256, Tomales, California 94971

Printed on recycled, permanent paper

∞

The paper used in this publication meets the minimum
requirements of American National Standard for Information
Services – Permanence of Paper for Printed Library Materials,
ANSI Z39.48-1984.

Acknowledgments are on page 201,
which constitues an extension of copyright page.

Library of Congress Cataloging-in-Publication Data
is on the last page of this book.

Table of Contents

Detailed Contents

Part One

Part Two

Part Three

Part Four

Part Five

EKNATH EASWARAN
About This Book

This book is a very personal one, and unlike any other collection of spiritual literature I have seen. It itself is rather
like a river, flowing through a country which is home for
all of us but which very, very few have seen: the land of
unity, in which all of creation is one and full of God.

There are no boundaries in this land. Those who dwell
in it live in a timeless realm beyond distinctions like time,
nationality, and language. So in the flow of this book, you
will encounter them without regard to such distinctions:
Mahatma Gandhi in the company of Saint Teresa of Avila
and the Compassionate Buddha, Rabbi Abraham Isaac
Kook next to Thomas a Kempis, David the Psalmist side
by side with the anonymous composer of the Katha Upanishad. They are listed by religious tradition at the end of
the book, where you will also find brief notes about each
mystic and scripture represented here.

There is one other difference between this book and
others I have seen: in addition to being a collection of in-
spiring spiritual literature, *God Makes the Rivers to Flow* is
an instrument for transforming one's life. I have taught
meditation for more than thirty years, and in this book I
have collected passages for meditation which, as I can testify from my own experience, have the power to remake
personality in the image of one's highest ideals. If this
appeals to you, everything you need to start is here.

I have read these passages countless times over the years,
yet I never tire of them. With every encounter I find deeper
meaning. May you, too, find in them a river of inspiration
that flows without end!

Introduction

In ancient India lived a sculptor renowned for his life-sized statues of elephants. With trunks curled high, tusks thrust forward, thick legs trampling the earth, these carved beasts seemed to trumpet to the sky. One day, a king came to see these magnificent works and to commission statuary for his palace. Struck with wonder, he asked the sculptor, "What is the secret of your artistry?"

The sculptor quietly took his measure of the monarch and replied, "Great king, when, with the aid of many men, I quarry a gigantic piece of granite from the banks of the river, I have it set here in my courtyard. For a long time I do nothing but observe this block of stone and study it from every angle. I focus all my concentration on this task and won't allow anything or anybody to disturb me. At first, I see nothing but a huge and shapeless rock sitting there, meaningless, indifferent to my purposes, utterly out of place. It seems faintly resentful at having been dragged from its cool place by the rushing waters. Then, slowly, very slowly, I begin to notice something in the substance of the rock. I feel a presentiment . . . an outline, scarcely discernible, shows itself to me, though others, I suspect, would perceive nothing. I watch with an open eye and a joyous, eager heart. The outline grows stronger. Oh, yes, I can see it! An elephant is stirring in there!

"Only then do I start to work. For days flowing into weeks, I use my chisel and mallet, always clinging to my sense of that outline, which grows ever stronger. How the big fellow strains! How he yearns to be out! How he wants to live! It seems so clear now, for I know the one thing I must do: with an utter singleness of purpose, I must chip away every last bit of stone that is not elephant. What then remains will be, must be, elephant."

When I was young, my grandmother, my spiritual guide, would often tell just such a story, not only to entertain but to convey the essential truths of living. Perhaps I had asked her, as revered teachers in every religion have been asked, "What happens in the spiritual life? What are we supposed to do?"

My granny wasn't a theologian, so she answered these questions simply with a story like that of the elephant sculptor. She was showing that we do not need to bring our real self, our higher self, into existence. It is already there. It has always been there, yearning to be out. An incomparable spark of divinity is to be found in the heart of each human being, waiting to radiate love and wisdom everywhere, because that is its nature. Amazing! This you that sometimes feels inadequate, sometimes becomes afraid or angry or depressed, that searches on and on for fulfillment, contains within itself the very fulfillment it seeks, and to a supreme degree.

Indeed, the tranquility and happiness we also feel are actually reflections of that inner reality of which we know so little. No matter what mistakes we may have made – and who hasn't made them? – this true self is ever pure and unsullied. No matter what trouble we have caused ourselves and those around us, this true self is ceaselessly loving. No matter how time passes from us and, with it, the body in which we dwell, this true self is beyond change, eternal.

Once we have become attentive to the presence of this true self, then all we really need do is resolutely chip away whatever is not divine in ourselves. I am not saying this is easy or quick. Quite the contrary; it can't be done in a week or by the weak. But the task is clearly laid out before us. By removing that which is petty and self-seeking, we bring forth all that is glorious and mindful of the whole. In this there is no loss, only gain. The chips pried away are of no consequence when compared to the magnificence of what will emerge. Can you imagine a sculptor scurrying to pick up the slivers that fall from his chisel, hoarding them, treasuring them, ignoring the statue altogether? Just so, when we get even a glimpse of the splendor of our inner being, our beloved preoccupations, predilections, and peccadillos will lose their glamour and seem utterly drab.

What remains when all that is not divine drops away is summed up in the short Sanskrit word *aroga*. The prefix *a* signifies "not a trace of "; *roga* means "illness" or "incapacity." Actually, the word loses some of its thrust in translation. In the original it connotes perfect well-being, not mere freedom from sickness. Often, you know, we say "I'm well" when all we mean is that we haven't taken to our bed with a bottle of cough syrup, a vaporizer, and a pitcher of fruit juice – we're getting about, more or less. But perhaps we have been so far from optimum functioning for so long that we don't realize what splendid health we are capable of. This *aroga* of the spiritual life entails the complete removal of every obstacle to impeccable health, giving us a strong and energetic body, a clear mind, positive emotions, and a heart radiant with love. When we have such soundness, we are always secure, always considerate, good to be around. Our relationships flourish, and we become a boon to the earth, not a burden on it.

Every time I reflect on this, I am filled with wonder. Voices can be heard crying out that human nature is debased, that everything is meaningless, that there is nothing we can do, but the mystics of every religion testify otherwise. They assure us that in every country, under adverse circumstances and favorable, ordinary people like you and me have taken on the immense challenge of the spiritual life and made this supreme discovery. They have found out who awaits them within the body, within the mind, within the human spirit. Consider the case of Francis Bernadone, who lived in Italy in the thirteenth century. I'm focusing on him because we know that, at the beginning, he was quite an ordinary young man. By day this son of a rich cloth merchant, a bit of a popinjay, lived the life of the privileged, with its games, its position, its pleasures. By night, feeling all the vigor of youth, he strolled the streets of Assisi with his lute, crooning love ballads beneath candle-lit balconies. Life was sweet, if shallow. But then the same force, the same dazzling inner light, that cast Saul of Tarsus to the earth and made him cry out, "Not I! Not I! But Christ liveth in me!" – just such a force plunges our troubadour deep within, wrenching loose all his old ways. He hears the irresistible voice of his God calling to him through a crucifix, "Francis, Francis, rebuild my church." And this meant not only the Chapel of San Damiano that lay in ruins nearby, not only the whole of the Church, but that which was closest of all – the man himself.

This tremendous turnabout in consciousness is compressed into the Prayer of Saint Francis. Whenever we repeat it, we are immersing ourselves in the spiritual wisdom of a holy lifetime. Here is the opening:

> Lord, make me an instrument of thy peace.
> Where there is hatred, let me sow love.

These lines are so deep that no one will ever fathom them. Profound, bottomless, they express the infinity of the Self. As you grow spiritually, they will mean more and more to you, without end.

But a very practical question arises here. Even if we recognize their great depth, we all know how terribly difficult it is to practice them in the constant give-and-take of life. For more than twenty years I have heard people, young and old, say that they respond to such magnificent words – that is just how they would like to be – but they don't know how to do it; it seems so far beyond their reach. In the presence of such spiritual wisdom, we feel so frail, so driven by personal concerns that we think we can never, never become like Saint Francis of Assisi.

I say to them, "There is a way." I tell them that we can change all that is selfish in us into selfless, all that is impure in us into pure, all that is unsightly into beauty. Happily, whatever our tradition, we are inheritors of straightforward spiritual practices whose power can be proved by anyone. These practices vary a bit from culture to culture, as you would expect, but essentially they are the same. Such practices are our sculptor's tools for carving away what is not-us so the real us can emerge.

Meditation is supreme among all these tested means for personal change. Nothing is so direct, so potent, so sure for releasing the divinity within us. Meditation enables us to see the lineaments of our true self and to chip away the stubbornly selfish tendencies that keep it locked within, quite, quite forgotten.

In meditation, the inspirational passage is the chisel, our concentration is the hammer, and our resolute will delivers the blows. And how the pieces fly! A very small, fine chisel edge, as you know, can wedge away huge chunks of stone. As with the other basic human tools – the lever, the pulley – we gain tremendous advantages of force. When we use our will to drive the thin edge of the passage deep into consciousness, we get the purchase to pry loose tenacious habits and negative attitudes. The passage, whether it is from the Bhagavad Gita or *The Imitation of Christ* or the Dhammapada of the Buddha, has been tempered in the flames of mystical experience, and its bite will . . . well, try it and find out for yourself just what it can do. In the end, only such personal experience persuades.

Now if we could hold an interview with a negative tendency, say, Resentment, it might say, "I don't worry! I've been safely settled in this fellow's mind for years. He takes good care of me – feeds me, dwells on me, brings me out and parades me around! All I have to do is roar and stir things up from time to time. Yes, I'm getting huge and feeling grand. And I'm proud to tell you there are even a few little rancors and vituperations running around now, spawned by yours truly!" So he may think. But I assure you that when you meditate on the glorious words of Saint Francis, you are prying him loose. You are saying in a way that goes beyond vows and good intentions that resentment is no part of you. You no longer acknowledge its right to exist. Thus, we bring ever more perceptibly into view our divine self. We use something genuine to drive out impostors that have roamed about largely through our neglect and helplessness.

To meditate and live the spiritual life we needn't drop everything and undertake an ascent of the Himalayas or Mount Athos or Cold Mountain. There are some who like to imagine themselves as pilgrims moving among the deer on high forest paths, simply-clad, sipping only pure headwaters, breathing only ethereal mountain air. Now it may sound unglamorous, but you can actually do better right where you are. Your situation may lack the grandeur of those austere and solitary peaks, but it could be a very fertile valley yielding marvelous fruit. We need people if we are to grow, and all our problems with them, properly seen, are opportunities for growth. Can you practice patience with a deer? Can you learn to forgive a redwood? But trying to live in harmony with those around you right now will bring out enormous inner toughness. Your powerful elephant will stir and come to life.

The old dispute about the relative virtues of the active way and the contemplative way is a spurious one. We require both. They are phases of a single rhythm like the pulsing of the heart, the in-drawing and letting go of breath, the ebb and flow of the tides. So we go deep, deep inwards in meditation to consolidate our vital energy, and then, with greater love and wisdom, we come out into the family, the community, the world. Without action we lack opportunities for changing our old ways, and we increase our self-will rather than lessen it; without contemplation, we lack the strength to change and are blown about by our conditioning. When we meditate every day and also do our best in every situation, we walk both worthy roads, the *via contemplativa* and the *via activa*.

The passages in this book are meant for meditation. So used, they can lead us deep into our minds where the transformation of all that is selfish in us must take place. Simply reading them may console us, it may inspire us, but it cannot bring about fundamental, lasting change; meditation alone does that. Only meditation, so far as I know, can release the inner resources locked within us, and put before us problems worthy of those resources. Only meditation gives such a vital edge to life. This is maturity. This is coming into our own, as our concerns deepen and broaden, dwarfing the personal satisfactions – and worries – that once meant so much to us.

If you want to know how to use inspirational passages in meditation, please read the instructions on page 183 of this book. The basic technique, duration and pace, posture, and place are all taken up. You will also find there the outline of a complete eight-point program for spiritual living, including the use of the mantram, slowing down, and achieving one-pointed attention. For a more detailed introduction to this program of self-transformation, I refer you to my other books, especially *Meditation*. I would like here, though, to say a bit about the criteria I have used in selecting these particular passages.

We wouldn't use a dull chisel or one meant for wood on a piece of stone, and we should use suitable passages for meditation. We're not after intellectual knowledge, which helps us understand and manipulate the external world. We seek spiritual wisdom, which leads to inner awareness. There, the separate strands of the external world – the people, the beasts and birds and fish, the trees and grasses, the moving waters and still, the earth itself – are brought into one great interconnected chord of life, and we find the will to live in accordance with that awareness. We find the will to live in perpetual love. I think you'll agree there are very few books which can ever lead us to that.

The test of suitable meditation passages is simply this: Does the passage bear the imprint of deep, personal spiritual experience? Is it the statement of one who went beyond the narrow confines of past conditioning into the unfathomable recesses of the mind, there to begin the great work of transformation? This is the unmistakable stamp of authenticity. Only such precious writings can speak directly to our heart and soul. Their very words are invested with validity; we feel we are in the presence of the genuine.

The scriptures of the world's religions certainly meet this test, and so do the statements of passionate lovers of God like Saint Teresa, Kabir, Sri Ramakrishna, Ansari of Herat. And whatever lacks this validation by personal experience, however poetic or imaginative, however speculative or novel, is not suited for use in meditation.

But there is another thing to be considered: Is the passage positive, inspirational, life-affirming? We should avoid passages from whatever source that are negative, that stress our foolish errors rather than our enduring strength and wisdom, or that deprecate life in the world, which is precisely where we must do our living. Instead, let us choose passages that hold steadily before us a radiant image of the true Self we are striving to realize.

For the great principle upon which meditation rests is that we become what we meditate on. Actually, even in everyday life, we are shaped by what gains our attention and occupies our thoughts. If we spend time studying the market, checking the money rates, evaluating our portfolios, we are going to become money-people. Anyone looking sensitively into our eyes will see two big dollar signs, and we'll look out at the world through them, too. Attention can be caught in so many things: food, books, collections, travel, television. The Buddha put it succinctly: "All that we are is the result of what we have thought."

If this is true of daily life, it is even more so in meditation, which is concentration itself. In the hours spent in meditation, we are removing many years of the "what we have thought." At that time, we need the most powerful tools we can find for accomplishing the task. That is why, in selecting passages, I have aimed for the highest the human being is capable of, the most noble and elevating truths that have ever been expressed on this planet. Our petty selfishness, our vain illusions, simply must and will give way under the power of these universal principles of life, as sand castles erode before the surge of the sea.

Specifically, what happens in meditation is that we slow down the furious, fragmented activity of the mind and lead it to a measured, sustained focus on what we want to become. Under the impact of a rapidly-moving, conditioned mind, we lose our sense of freely choosing. But, as the mind slows down, we begin to gain control of it in daily life. Many habitual responses in what we eat, see, and do, and in the ways we relate to people, come under our inspection and governance. We realize that we have choices. This is profoundly liberating and takes away every trace of boredom and depression.

The passages in this collection have been drawn from many traditions, and you'll find considerable variety among them. Some are in verse, some in prose; some are from the East, some from the West; some are ancient, some quite recent; some stress love, some insight, some good works. So there are differences, yes, in tone, theme, cultural milieu, but they all have this in common: they will work.

As your meditation progresses, I encourage you to build a varied repertory of passages to guard against overfamiliarity, where the repetition can become somewhat mechanical. In this way, you can match a passage to your particular need at the time – the inspiration, the reminder, the reassurance most meaningful to you.

Nearly everyone has had some longing to be an artist and can feel some affinity with my granny's elephant sculptor. Most of us probably spent some time at painting, writing, dancing, or music-making. Whether it has fallen away, or we still keep our hand in, we remember our touches with the great world of art, a world of beauty and harmony, of similitudes and stark contrasts, of repetition and variation, of compelling rhythms like those of the cosmos itself. We know, too, that while we can all appreciate art, only a few can create masterworks or perform them as virtuosi.

Now I wish to invite you to undertake the greatest art work of all, an undertaking which is for everyone, forever, never to be put aside, even for a single day. I speak of the purpose of life, the thing without which every other goal or achievement will lose its meaning and turn to ashes. I invite you to step back and look with your artist's eye at your own life. Consider it amorphous material, not yet deliberately crafted. Reflect upon what it is, and what it could be. Imagine how you will feel, and what those around you will lose, if it does not become what it could be. Observe that you have been given two marvelous instruments of love and service: the external instrument, this intricate network of systems that is the body; the internal, this subtle and versatile mind. Ponder the deeds they have given rise to, and the deeds they can give rise to.

And set to work. Sit for meditation, and sit again. Every day without fail, sick or well, tired or energetic, alone or with others, at home or away from home, sit for meditation, as great artists throw themselves into their creations. As you sit, you will have in hand the supreme hammer and chisel; use it to hew away all unwanted effects of your heredity, conditioning, environment, and latencies. Bring forth the noble work of art within you! My earnest wish is that one day you shall see, in all its purity, the effulgent spiritual being you really are.

May the river of my life
flow into the sea of love
that is the Lord.

Part One

The Prayer of Saint Francis

Lord, make me an instrument of thy peace.
Where there is hatred, let me sow love;
Where there is injury, pardon;
Where there is doubt, faith;
Where there is despair, hope;
Where there is darkness, light;
Where there is sadness, joy.

O divine Master, grant that I may not so much seek
To be consoled as to console,
To be understood as to understand,
To be loved as to love;
For it is in giving that we receive;
It is in pardoning that we are pardoned;
It is in dying to self that we are born to eternal life.

Invocations

Lead me from the unreal to the real.
Lead me from darkness to light.
Lead me from death to immortality.

1

May the Lord of Love protect us.
May the Lord of Love nourish us.
May the Lord of Love strengthen us.
May we realize the Lord of Love.
May we live with love for all;
May we live in peace with all.
O M *Shanti Shanti Shanti*

2

May the Lord of day grant us peace.
May the Lord of night grant us peace.
May the Lord of sight grant us peace.
May the Lord of might grant us peace.
May the Lord of speech grant us peace.
May the Lord of space grant us peace.
I bow down to Brahman, source of all power.
I will speak the truth and follow the law.
Guard me and my teacher against all harm.
Guard me and my teacher against all harm.
O M *Shanti Shanti Shanti*

3

Filled with Brahman are the things we see,
Filled with Brahman are the things we see not,
From out of Brahman floweth all that is:
From Brahman all – yet is he still the same.
O M *Shanti Shanti Shanti*

4

May quietness descend upon my limbs,
My speech, my breath, my eyes, my ears;
May all my senses wax clear and strong.
May Brahman show himself unto me.
Never may I deny Brahman, nor Brahman me.
I with him and he with me –
    may we abide always together.
May there be revealed to me,
Who am devoted to Brahman,
The holy truth of the Upanishads.
   O M *Shanti Shanti Shanti*

5

   O M
With our ears may we hear what is good.
With our eyes may we behold thy righteousness.
Tranquil in body, may we who worship thee
    find rest.
    O M *Shanti Shanti Shanti*
    O M . . . *Hail to the supreme Self!*

May my speech be one with my mind,
and may my mind be one with my speech.
O thou self-luminous Brahman,
remove the veil of ignorance from before me,
that I may behold thy light.
Do thou reveal to me
the spirit of the scriptures.
May the truth of the scriptures
be ever present to me.
May I seek day and night to realize
what I learn from the sages.
May I speak the truth of Brahman.
May I speak the truth.
May it protect me.
May it protect my teacher.
O M *Shanti Shanti Shanti*

The Shema

Hear, O Israel,
the Lord our God, the Lord is one.
Blessed is his name,
whose glorious kingdom is forever.

And you shall love the Lord with all your heart, and with all your soul, and with all your might.

And these words, which I command you this day, shall be upon your heart: and you shall teach them always to your children, and shall talk of them when you sit in your house, when you walk by the way, when you lie down, and when you arise.

And you shall bind them as a sign on your hand, and they will be seen as a badge between your eyes.

And you shall write them on the doorposts of your house, and upon your gates.

Hymn to the Divine Mother

O thou the giver of all blessings,
O thou the doer of all good,
O thou the fulfiller of all desires,
O thou the giver of refuge –
Our salutations to thee, O Mother Divine.

O thou Eternal Mother,
Thou hast the power to create, to preserve,
    and to dissolve.
Thou the dwelling-place and embodiment
    of the three gunas –
Our salutations to thee, O Mother Divine.

O thou the savior of all who take refuge in thee,
The lowly and the distressed –
O Mother Divine, we salute thee,
Who takest away the sufferings of all.

The Illumined Man

ARJUNA:
Tell me of the man who lives in wisdom,
Ever aware of the Self, O Krishna;
How does he talk, how sit, how move about?

SRI KRISHNA:
He lives in wisdom
Who sees himself in all and all in him,
Whose love for the Lord of Love has consumed
Every selfish desire and sense-craving
Tormenting the heart. Not agitated
By grief nor hankering after pleasure,
He lives free from lust and fear and anger.
Fettered no more by selfish attachments,
He is not elated by good fortune
Nor depressed by bad. Such is the seer.

Even as a tortoise draws in its limbs
The sage can draw in his senses at will.
An aspirant abstains from sense-pleasures,
But he still craves for them. These cravings all
Disappear when he sees the Lord of Love.
For even of one who treads the path
The stormy senses can sweep off the mind.
But he lives in wisdom who subdues them,
And keeps his mind ever absorbed in me.

When you keep thinking about sense-objects,
Attachment comes. Attachment breeds desire,

The lust of possession which, when thwarted,
Burns to anger. Anger clouds the judgment
And robs you of the power to learn from past mistakes.
Lost is the discriminative faculty,
And your life is utter waste.

But when you move amidst the world of sense
From both attachment and aversion freed,
There comes the peace in which all sorrows end,
And you live in the wisdom of the Self.

The disunited mind is far from wise;
How can it meditate? How be at peace?
When you know no peace, how can you know joy?
When you let your mind follow the Siren call
Of the senses, they carry away
Your better judgment as a cyclone drives a boat
Off the charted course to its doom.

Use your mighty arms to free the senses
From attachment and aversion alike,
And live in the full wisdom of the Self.
Such a sage awakes to light in the night
Of all creatures. Wherein they are awake
Is the night of ignorance to the sage.

As the rivers flow into the ocean
But cannot make the vast ocean o'erflow,
So flow the magic streams of the sense-world
Into the sea of peace that is the sage.

He is forever free who has broken out
Of the ego-cage of *I* and *mine*
To be united with the Lord of Love.
This is the supreme state. Attain thou this
And pass from death to immortality.

Finding Unity

Those who know do not speak;
Those who speak do not know.
Stop up the openings,
Close down the doors,
Rub off the sharp edges.
Unravel all confusion.
Harmonize the light,
Give up contention:
This is called finding the unity of life.

When love and hatred cannot affect you,
Profit and loss cannot touch you,
Praise and blame cannot ruffle you,
You are honored by all the world.

I Gave All My Heart

I gave all my heart to the Lord of Love,
And my life is so completely transformed
That my Beloved One has become mine
And without a doubt I am his at last.

When that tender hunter from paradise
Released his piercing arrow at me,
My wounded soul fell in his loving arms;
And my life is so completely transformed
That my Beloved One has become mine
And without a doubt I am his at last.

He pierced my heart with his arrow of love
And made me one with the Lord who made me.
This is the only love I have to prove,
And my life is so completely transformed
That my Beloved One has become mine
And without a doubt I am his at last.

Prayers

1

May we be united in heart.
May we be united in speech.
May we be united in mind.
May we perform our duties
As did the wise of old.

May we be united in our prayer.
May we be united in our goal.
May we be united in our resolve.
May we be united in our understanding.
May we be united in our offering.
May we be united in our feelings.
May we be united in our hearts.
May we be united in our thoughts.
May there be perfect unity amongst us.

God makes the rivers to flow. They tire not, nor
do they cease from flowing. May the river of my life flow
into the sea of love that is the Lord.

May I overcome all the impediments in my course. May
the thread of my song be not cut before my life merges in
the sea of love.

Guard me against all danger, O Lord. Accept me
graciously, O King of kings.

Release me from my sorrows, which hold me as ropes
hold a calf. I cannot even open my eyes without the
power of your love.

Guard us against the grief that haunts the life of the
selfish. Lead us from darkness into light.

We will sing of your love as it was sung of old. Your laws
change not, but stand like the mountains.

Forgive me all the mistakes I have committed. Many
mornings will dawn upon us again. Guide us through
them all, O Lord of Love.

The Miracle of Illumination

As a blind man feels when he finds a pearl in a dustbin, so am I amazed by the miracle of Bodhi rising in my consciousness. It is the nectar of immortality that delivers us from death, the treasure that lifts us above poverty into the wealth of giving to life, the tree that gives shade to us when we roam about scorched by life, the bridge that takes us across the stormy river of life, the cool moon of compassion that calms our mind when it is agitated, the sun that dispels darkness, the butter made from the milk of kindness by churning it with the dharma. It is a feast of joy to which all are invited.

Twin Verses

Our life is shaped by our mind; we become what we think. Suffering follows an evil thought as the wheels of a cart follow the oxen that draw it.
Our life is shaped by our mind; we become what we think. Joy follows a pure thought like a shadow that never leaves.

★

"He was angry with me, he attacked me, he defeated me, he robbed me" – those who dwell on such thoughts will never be free from hatred.
"He was angry with me, he attacked me, he defeated me, he robbed me" – those who do not dwell on such thoughts will surely become free from hatred.

★

For hatred can never put an end to hatred; love alone can. This is an unalterable law.
People forget that their lives will end soon. For those who remember, quarrels come to an end.

★

As a strong wind blows down a weak-rooted tree, Mara the Tempter overwhelms weak people who, eating too much and working too little, are caught in the frantic pursuit of pleasure.

As the strongest wind cannot shake a mountain, Mara cannot shake those who are self-disciplined and full of faith.

★

Those who put on the saffron robe without purifying the mind, who lack truthfulness and self-control, are not fit to wear this sacred garment.
But those who have purified their minds and are endowed with truth and self-control are truly fit to wear the saffron robe.

★

The deluded, imagining trivial things to be vital to life, follow their vain fancies and never attain the highest knowledge.
But the wise, knowing what is trivial and what is vital, set their thoughts on the supreme goal and attain the highest knowledge.

★

As rain seeps through an ill-thatched hut, passion will seep through an untrained mind.
As rain cannot seep through a well-thatched hut, passion cannot seep through a well-trained mind.

★

Those who are selfish suffer here and hereafter; they suffer in both worlds from the results of their own actions.
But those who are selfless rejoice here and rejoice hereafter; they rejoice in both worlds from the results of their own actions.

★

Those who are selfish suffer in this life and in the next.
They suffer seeing the results of the evil they have done,
and more suffering awaits them in the next life.
But those who are selfless rejoice in this life and in the
next. They rejoice seeing the good that they have done,
and more joy awaits them in the next life.

★

Those who recite many scriptures but fail to practice
their teachings are like a cowherd counting another's
cows. They do not share in the joys of the spiritual life.
But those who know few scriptures but practice their
teachings, overcoming all lust, hatred, and delusion, live
with a pure mind in the highest wisdom. They stand
without external supports and share in the joys of the
spiritual life.

The Wonderful Effects of Divine Love

1

Ah, Lord God, thou holy lover of my soul, when thou comest into my heart, all that is within me shall rejoice.

Thou art my glory and the exultation of my heart: thou art my hope and refuge in the day of my trouble.

2

But because I am as yet weak in love, and imperfect in virtue, I have need to be strengthened and comforted by thee; visit me therefore often, and instruct me with all holy discipline.

Set me free from evil passions, and heal my heart of all inordinate affections; that being inwardly cured and thoroughly cleansed, I may be made fit to love, courageous to suffer, steady to persevere.

3

Love is a great thing, yea, a great and thorough good; by itself it makes every thing that is heavy, light; and it bears evenly all that is uneven.

For it carries a burden which is no burden, and makes every thing that is bitter, sweet and tasteful.

The noble love of Jesus impels one to do great things, and stirs one up to be always longing for what is more perfect.

Love desires to be aloft, and will not be kept back by any thing low and mean.

Love desires to be free, and estranged from all worldly affections, that so its inward sight may not be hindered; that it may not be entangled by any temporal prosperity, or by any adversity subdued.

Nothing is sweeter than love, nothing more courageous, nothing higher, nothing wider, nothing more pleasant, nothing fuller nor better in heaven and earth; because love is born of God, and cannot rest but in God, above all created things.

4

He that loveth, flyeth, runneth, and rejoiceth; he is free, and cannot be held in.

He giveth all for all, and hath all in all; because he resteth in One highest above all things, from whom all that is good flows and proceeds.

He respecteth not the gifts, but turneth himself above all goods unto the Giver.

Love often times knoweth no measure, but is fervent beyond all measure.

Love feels no burden, thinks nothing of trouble, attempts what is above its strength, pleads no excuse of impossibility; for it thinks all things lawful for itself and all things possible.

It is therefore able to undertake all things, and it completes many things, and warrants them to take effect, where he who does not love, would faint and lie down.

5

Love is watchful, and sleeping slumbereth not.

Though weary, it is not tired; though pressed, it is not straitened; though alarmed, it is not confounded; but as a lively flame and burning torch, it forces its way upwards, and securely passes through all.

If any one love, he knoweth what is the cry of this voice. For it is a loud cry in the ears of God, the mere ardent affection of the soul, when it saith, "My God, my love, thou art all mine, and I am all thine."

6

Enlarge thou me in love, that with the inward palate of my heart I may taste how sweet it is to love, and to be dissolved, and as it were to bathe myself in thy love.

Let me be possessed by love, mounting above myself, through excessive fervor and admiration.

Let me sing the song of love, let me follow thee, my Beloved, on high; let my soul spend itself in thy praise, rejoicing through love.

Let me love thee more than myself, nor love myself but for thee: and in thee all that truly love thee, as the law of love commandeth, shining out from thyself.

7

Love is active, sincere, affectionate, pleasant and amiable; courageous, patient, faithful, prudent, long-suffering, resolute, and never seeking itself.

For in whatever instance one seeketh oneself, there he falleth from love.

Love is circumspect, humble, and upright: not yielding to softness, or to levity, nor attending to vain things; it is sober, chaste, steady, quiet, and guarded in all the senses.

Love is subject, and obedient to its superiors, to itself mean and despised, unto God devout and thankful, trusting and hoping always in Him, even then when God imparteth no relish of sweetness unto it: for without sorrow, none liveth in love.

8

He that is not prepared to suffer all things, and to stand to the will of his Beloved, is not worthy to be called a lover of God.

A lover ought to embrace willingly all that is hard and distasteful, for the sake of his Beloved; and not to turn away from him for any contrary accidents.

The Real Lovers of God

They are the real lovers of God
Who feel others' sorrow as their own.
When they perform selfless service,
They are humble servants of the Lord.
Respecting all, despising none,
They are pure in thought, word, and deed.
Blessed is the mother of such a child;
And in their eyes the Divine Mother
Shines in every woman they see.
They are always truthful, even-minded,
Never coveting others' wealth,
Free from all selfish attachments,
Ever in tune with the Holy Name.
Their bodies are like sacred shrines
In which the Lord of Love is seen.
Free from greed, anger, and fear,
These are the real lovers of God.

Only God I Saw

In the market, in the cloister – only God I saw.
In the valley and on the mountain – only God I saw.

Him I have seen beside me oft in tribulation;
In favor and in fortune – only God I saw.

In prayer and fasting, in praise and contemplation,
In the religion of the Prophet – only God I saw.

Neither soul nor body, accident nor substance,
Qualities nor causes – only God I saw.

I oped mine eyes and by the light of his face around me
In all the eye discovered – only God I saw.

Like a candle I was melting in his fire:
Amidst the flames outflashing – only God I saw.

Myself with mine own eyes I saw most clearly,
But when I looked with God's eyes – only God I saw.

I passed away into nothingness, I vanished,
And lo, I was the All-living – only God I saw.

Perennial Joy

THE KING OF DEATH:
The joy of the spirit ever abides,
But not what seems pleasant to the senses.
Both these, differing in their purpose, prompt us
To action. All is well for those who choose
The joy of the spirit, but they miss
The goal of life who prefer the pleasant.
Perennial joy or passing pleasure?
This is the choice one is to make always.
The wise recognize this; the ignorant
Do not. The first welcome what leads to joy
Abiding, even though painful at the time.
The latter run, goaded by their senses,
After what seems immediate pleasure.

Well have you renounced these passing pleasures
So dear to the senses, Nachiketa,
And turned your back on the way of the world
Which makes mankind forget the goal of life.

Far apart are wisdom and ignorance:
The first leads one to Self-realization;
The second makes one more and more
Estranged from one's real Self. I regard you,
Nachiketa, as worthy of instruction,
For passing pleasures tempt you not at all.

Ignorant of their ignorance yet wise
In their own esteem, deluded people
Proud of their vain learning go round and round
Like the blind led by the blind. Far beyond
Their eyes, hypnotized by the world of sense,
Opens the way to immortality.
"I am my body; when my body dies,
I die." Living in this superstition they fall,
Life after life, under my sway.

It is but few who hear about the Self.
Fewer still dedicate their lives to its
Realization. Wonderful is the one
Who speaks of the Self. Rare are they
Who make it the supreme goal of their life.
Blessed are they who, through an illumined
Teacher, attain to Self-realization.

The truth of the Self cannot come through one
Who has not realized that he is the Self.
The intellect can never reach the Self,
Beyond its duality of subject
And object. He who sees himself in all
And all in him helps one through spiritual
Osmosis to realize the Self oneself.
This awakening you have known comes not
Through logic and scholarship, but from
Close association with a realized teacher.
Wise are you, Nachiketa, because you
Seek the Self eternal. May we have more
Seekers like you!

NACHIKETA:
I know that earthly treasures are transient,
And never can I reach the Eternal
Through them. Hence have I renounced

All the desires of Nachiketa for earthly treasures
To win the Eternal through your instruction.

THE KING OF DEATH:
I spread before your eyes, Nachiketa,
The fulfillment of all worldly desires:
Power to dominate the earth, delights
Celestial gained through religious rites, and
Miraculous powers beyond time and space.
These with will and wisdom have you renounced.

The wise, realizing through meditation
The timeless Self, beyond all perception,
Hidden in the cave of the heart,
Leave pain and pleasure far behind.
Those who know that they are neither body
Nor mind but the immemorial Self,
The divine principle of existence,
Find the source of all joy and live in joy
Abiding. I see the gates of joy
Are opening for you, Nachiketa.

NACHIKETA:
Teach me of That you see as beyond right
And wrong, cause and effect, past and future.

THE KING OF DEATH:
I will give you the Word all the scriptures
Glorify, all spiritual disciplines
Express, to attain which aspirants lead
A life of sense-restraint and self-naughting.
It is O M. This symbol of the Godhead
Is the highest. Realizing it, one finds
Complete fulfillment of all one's longings.
It is the greatest support to all seekers.
When O M reverberates unceasingly

Within one's heart, that one is indeed blessed
And greatly loved as one who is the Self.

The all-knowing Self was never born,
Nor will it die. Beyond cause and effect,
This Self is eternal and immutable.
When the body dies, the Self does not die.
If the slayer believes that he can kill
And the slain believes that he can be killed,
Neither knows the truth. The eternal Self
Slays not, nor is ever slain.

Hidden in the heart of every creature
Exists the Self, subtler than the subtlest,
Greater than the greatest. They go beyond
All sorrow who extinguish their self-will,
And behold the glory of the Self
Through the grace of the Lord of Love.

Though one sits in meditation in a
Particular place, the Self within can
Exercise its influence far away.
Though still, it moves everything everywhere.

When the wise realize the Self, formless
In the midst of forms, changeless in the midst
Of change, omnipresent and supreme,
They go beyond all sorrow.

The Self cannot be known through the study
Of the scriptures, nor through the intellect,
Nor through hearing discourses about it.
It can be attained only by those
Whom the Self chooses. Verily unto them
Does the Self reveal itself.

The Self cannot be known by anyone
Who desists not from unrighteous ways,
Controls not the senses, stills not the mind,
And practices not meditation.
None else can know the omnipresent Self,
Whose glory sweeps away the rituals of
The priest and the prowess of the warrior
And puts death itself to death.

Part Two

Adon Olam

The Lord of the universe
Ruled before creation.

When by his will all things came to be,
The name of the Lord was known.

As the Lord creates, he may end the creation,
Remaining alone, unmanifested.
He was, he is, and he shall remain eternal.

He is without beginning;
He is without end.

He is my God, my living strength,
My refuge when I grieve.
He is my only desire.
I live in him alone.

My soul abides in his hands
In sleep as in wakefulness.

Though I leave my body
I will not fear,
For the Lord is with my soul.

Discourse on Good Will

May all beings be filled with joy and peace.
May all beings everywhere,
The strong and the weak,
The great and the small,
The mean and the powerful,
The short and the long,
The subtle and the gross:

May all beings everywhere,
Seen and unseen,
Dwelling far off or nearby,
Being or waiting to become:
May all be filled with lasting joy.

Let no one deceive another,
Let no one anywhere despise another,
Let no one out of anger or resentment
Wish suffering on anyone at all.

Just as a mother with her own life
Protects her child, her only child, from harm,
So within yourself let grow
A boundless love for all creatures.

Let your love flow outward through the universe,
To its height, its depth, its broad extent,
A limitless love, without hatred or enmity.

Then, as you stand or walk,
Sit or lie down,
As long as you are awake,
Strive for this with a one-pointed mind;
Your life will bring heaven to earth.

The Central Truth

Forget not the central truth that God is seated in your own heart. Don't be disheartened by failures at initial stages. Cultivate the spirit of surrender to the workings of his will, inside you and outside you, until you have completely surrendered up your ego-sense and have known that he is in all, and he is all, and you and he are one. Be patient. The path of self-discipline that leads to God-realization is not an easy path: obstacles and sufferings are on the path; the latter you must bear, and the former overcome — all by his help. His help comes only through concentration. Repetition of God's name helps concentration.

The Whole World Is Your Own

I tell you one thing –
If you want peace of mind,
do not find fault with others.

Rather learn to see your own faults.
Learn to make the whole world your own.

No one is a stranger, my child;
this whole world is your own.

The Practice of the Presence of God

1

O my God, since thou art with me, and I must now, in obedience to thy commands, apply my mind to these out-ward things, I beseech thee to grant me the grace to con-tinue in thy presence; and to this end do thou prosper me with thy assistance, receive all my works, and possess all my affections.

2

God knoweth best what is needful for us, and all that he does is for our good. If we knew how much he loves us, we should always be ready to receive equally and with indifference from his hand the sweet and the bitter. All would please that came from him. The sorest afflictions never appear intolerable, except when we see them in the wrong light. When we see them as dispensed by the hand of God, when we know that it is our loving Father who abases and distresses us, our sufferings will lose their bitterness and become even matter of consolation.

Let all our employment be to know God; the more one knows him, the more one desires to know him. And as knowledge is commonly the measure of love, the deeper and more extensive our knowledge shall be, the greater will be our love; and if our love of God were great, we should love him equally in pains and pleasures.

Let us not content ourselves with loving God for the mere sensible favors, how elevated soever, which he has done or may do us. Such favors, though never so great, cannot bring us so near to him as faith does in one simple act. Let us seek him often by faith. He is within us; seek him not elsewhere. If we do love him alone, are we not rude, and do we not deserve blame, if we busy ourselves about trifles which do not please and perhaps offend him? It is to be feared these trifles will one day cost us dear.

Let us begin to be devoted to him in good earnest. Let us cast everything besides out of our hearts. He would possess them alone. Beg this favor of him. If we do what we can on our part, we shall soon see that change wrought in us which we aspire after.

Her Heart Is Full of Joy

Her heart is full of joy with love,
For in the Lord her mind is stilled.
She has renounced every selfish attachment
And draws abiding joy and strength
From the One within.
She lives not for herself, but lives
To serve the Lord of Love in all,
And swims across the sea of life
Breasting its rough waves joyfully.

The Razor's Edge

In the secret cave of the heart, two are
Seated by life's fountain. The separate ego
Drinks of the sweet and bitter stuff,
Liking the sweet, disliking the bitter,
While the supreme Self drinks sweet and bitter
Neither liking this nor disliking that.
The ego gropes in darkness, while the Self
Lives in light. So declare the illumined sages,
And the householders who worship
The sacred fire in the name of the Lord.

May we light the fire of Nachiketa
That burns out the ego, and enables us
To pass from fearful fragmentation
To fearless fullness in the changeless Whole.

Know the Self as lord of the chariot,
The body as the chariot itself,
The discriminating intellect as
The charioteer, and the mind as the reins.
The senses, say the wise, are the horses;
Selfish desires are the roads they travel.
When the Self is confused with the body,
Mind, and senses, they point out, he seems
To enjoy pleasure and suffer sorrow.

When a person lacks discrimination
And his mind is undisciplined, his senses
Run hither and thither like wild horses.

But they obey the rein like trained horses
When a person has discrimination
And the mind is one-pointed. Those who lack
Discrimination, with little control
Over their thoughts and far from pure,
Reach not the pure state of immortality
But wander from death to death; while those
Who have discrimination, with a still mind
And a pure heart, reach journey's end,
Never again to fall into the jaws of death.
With a discriminating intellect
As charioteer, a well-trained mind as reins,
They attain the supreme goal of life
To be united with the Lord of Love.

The senses derive from objects of sense-perception,
Sense-objects from mind, mind from intellect,
And intellect from ego; ego from undifferentiated
Consciousness, and consciousness from Brahman.
Brahman is the first Cause and last refuge.
Brahman, the hidden Self in everyone,
Does not shine forth. He is revealed only
To those who keep their minds one-pointed
On the Lord of Love and thus develop
A superconscious manner of knowing.
Meditation empowers them to go
Deeper and deeper into consciousness,
From the world of words to the world of thought,
Then beyond thoughts to wisdom in the Self.

Get up! Wake up! Seek the guidance of an
Illumined teacher and realize the Self.
Sharp like a razor's edge is the path,
The sages say, difficult to traverse.

The supreme Self is beyond name and form,
Beyond the senses, inexhaustible,
Without beginning, without end,
Beyond time, space, and causality, eternal,
Immutable. Those who realize the Self
Are forever free from the jaws of death.

The wise, who gain experiential knowledge
Of this timeless tale of Nachiketa
Narrated by Death, attain the glory
Of living in spiritual awareness.
Those who, full of devotion, recite this
Supreme mystery at a spiritual
Gathering, are fit for eternal life.
They are indeed fit for eternal life.

Mother of All Things

The universe had a beginning
Called the Mother of All Things.
Once you have found the Mother
You can know her children.
Having known the children,
Hold tightly to the Mother.
Your whole life will be preserved from peril.

Open up the openings,
Multiply your affairs,
Your whole life will become a burden.

Those who see the small are called clear-headed;
Those who hold to gentleness are called strong.

Use the light.
Come home to your true nature.
Don't cause yourself injury:
This is known as seizing truth.

Invocations

In the name of God,
Most gracious,
Most merciful.

O thou munificent one
Who art the bestower of all bounties,
O thou wise one
Who overlookest our faults,
O self-existent one
Who art beyond our comprehension,
O thou omnipotent one
Who hast no equal in power and greatness,
Who art without a second:
O thou merciful one
Who guidest stray souls to the right path,
Thou art truly our God.

Give purity to our minds,
Aspiration to our hearts,
Light to our eyes.
Out of thy grace and bounty
Give us that which thou deemest best.

O Lord, out of thy grace
Give faith and light to our hearts,
And with the medicine of truth and steadfastness
Cure the ills of our life.

I know not what to ask of thee.
Thou art the knower;
Give what thou deemest best.

O God, may my brain reel with thoughts of thee,
May my heart thrill with the mysteries of thy grace,
May my tongue move only to utter thy praise.

I live only to do thy will;
My lips move only in praise of thee.
O Lord, whoever becometh aware of thee,
Casteth out all else other than thee.

O Lord, give me a heart
That I may pour it out in thanksgiving.
Give me life
That I may spend it in working
For the salvation of the world.

O Lord, give me that right discrimination
That the lure of the world may cheat me no more.
Give me strength
That my faith suffer no eclipse.

O Lord, give me understanding
That I stray not from the path.
Give me light
To avoid pitfalls.

O Lord, keep watch over me
That I stray not.
Keep me on the path of righteousness
That I escape from the pangs of repentance.

O Lord, judge me not by my actions.
Of thy mercy, save me,
And make my humble efforts fruitful.

O Lord, give me a heart
Free from the flames of desire.
Give me a mind
Free from the waves of egoism.

O Lord, give me eyes
Which see nothing but thy glory.
Give me a mind
That finds delight in thy service.
Give me a soul
Drunk in the wine of thy wisdom.

O Lord, to find thee is my desire,
But to comprehend thee is beyond my strength.
Remembering thee is solace to my sorrowing heart;
Thoughts of thee are my constant companions.
I call upon thee night and day.
The flame of thy love glows
In the darkness of my night.

Life in my body pulsates only for thee
My heart beats in resignation to thy will.
If on my dust a tuft of grass were to grow,
Every blade would tremble with my devotion for thee.

O Lord, everyone desires to behold thee.
I desire that thou mayest cast a glance at me.
Let me not disgrace myself.
If thy forgiveness awaits me in the end,
Lower not the standard of forgiveness
Which thou hast unfurled.

O Lord, prayer at thy gate
Is a mere formality:
Thou knowest what thy slave desires.
O Lord, better for me to be dust

And my name effaced
From the records of the world
Than that thou forget me.

He knoweth all our good and evil.
Nothing is hidden from him.
He knoweth what is the best medicine
To cure the pain and to rescue the fallen.
Be humble, for he exalteth the humble.

I am intoxicated with love for thee
And need no fermented wine.
I am thy bird, free from need of seed
And safe from the snare of the fowler.
In the kaaba and in the temple,
Thou art the object of my search.
Else I am freed
From both these places of worship.

Lord, when thou wert hidden from me
The fever of life possessed me.
When thou revealest thyself
This fever of life departeth.

O Lord, other men are afraid of thee
But I – I am afraid of myself.
From thee flows good alone,
From me flows evil.
Others fear what the morrow may bring;
I am afraid of what happened yesterday.

O Lord, if thou holdest me responsible for my sins
I shall cling to thee for thy grace.
I with my sin am an insignificant atom.
Thy grace is resplendent as the sun.

O Lord, out of regard for thy name,
The qualities which are thine,
Out of regard for thy greatness,
Listen to my cry,
For thou alone canst redeem me.

O Lord, intoxicate me with the wine of thy love.
Place the chains of thy slavery on my feet;
Make me empty of all but thy love,
And in it destroy me and bring me back to life.
The hunger thou has awakened
Culminates in fulfillment.

Make my body impervious to the fires of hell;
Vouchsafe to me a vision of thee in heaven.
The spark thou hast kindled, make it everlasting.

I think of no other,
And in thy love care for none else.
None has a place in my heart but thee.
My heart has become thy abode;
It has no place for another.

O Lord, thou cherishest the helpless,
And I am helpless.
Apply thy balm to my bleeding heart,
For thou art the physician.

O Lord, I, a beggar, ask of thee
More than what a thousand kings may ask of thee.
Each one has something he needs to ask of thee;
I have come to ask thee to give me thyself.

If words can establish a claim,
I claim a crown.
But if deeds are wanted,
I am as helpless as the ant.

Urged by desire, I wandered
In the streets of good and evil.
I gained nothing except feeding the fire of desire.
As long as in me remains the breath of life,
Help me, for thou alone canst hear my prayer.

Watch vigilantly the state of thine own mind.
Love of God begins in harmlessness.

Know that the prophet built an external kaaba
Of clay and water,
And an inner kaaba in life and heart.
The outer kaaba was built by Abraham, the holy;
The inner is sanctified by the glory of God himself.

On the path of God
Two places of worship mark the stages,
The material temple
And the temple of the heart.
Make your best endeavor
To worship at the temple of the heart.

In this path, be one
With a heart full of compassion.
Engage not in vain doing;
Make not thy home in the street of lust and desire.

If thou wouldst become a pilgrim on the path of love,
The first condition is that thou become
As humble as dust and ashes.

Know that when thou learnest to lose thy self
Thou wilt reach the Beloved.
There is no other secret to be revealed,
And more than this is not known to me.

Be humble and cultivate silence.
If thou hast received, rejoice,
And fill thyself with ecstasy.
And if not, continue the demand.

What is worship?
To realize reality.
What is the sacred law?
To do no evil.
What is reality?
Selflessness.

The heart inquired of the soul,
What is the beginning of this business?
What its end, and what its fruit?
The soul answered:
The beginning of it is the annihilation of self,
Its end faithfulness,
And its fruit immortality.

The heart asked, what is annihilation?
What is faithfulness?
What is immortality?
The soul answered:
Freedom from self is annihilation.
Faithfulness is fulfillment of love.
Immortality is the union of immortal with mortal.

In this path the eye must cease to see
And the ear to hear,
Save unto him and about him.
Be as dust on his path;
Even the kings of this earth
Make the dust of his feet
The balm of their eyes.

Simple Union

O seeker, the simple union is the best.
Since the day when I met with my Lord,
There has been no end to the sport of our love.
I shut not my eyes, I close not my ears,
I do not mortify my body; I see with eyes open
And smile and behold his beauty everywhere:
I utter his name, and whatever I see,
It reminds me of him; whatever I do,
It becomes his worship.
The rising and the setting are one to me:
All contradictions are solved.
Wherever I go, I move round him.
All I achieve is his service: when I lie down,
I lie prostrate at his feet.
He is the only adorable one to me:
I have none other.
My tongue has left off impure words;
It sings his glory, day and night.
Whether I rise or sit down, I can never forget him,
For the rhythm of his music beats in my ears.
Kabir says: My heart is frenzied
And I disclose in my soul what is hidden.
I am immersed in that great bliss
Which transcends all pleasure and pain.

The Way of Love

ARJUNA:

Of those who love you as the Lord of Love,
Ever present in all, and those who seek you
As the nameless, formless Reality,
Which way is sure and swift, love or knowledge?

SRI KRISHNA:

For those who set their hearts on me
And worship me with unfailing devotion and faith,
The way of love leads sure and swift to me.

Those who seek the transcendental Reality,
Unmanifested, without name or form,
Beyond the reach of feeling and of thought,
With their senses subdued and mind serene
And striving for the good of all beings,
They too will verily come unto me.

Yet hazardous
And slow is the path to the Unrevealed,
Difficult for physical man to tread.
But they for whom I am the goal supreme,
Who do all work renouncing self for me
And meditate on me with single-hearted devotion,
These will I swiftly rescue
From the fragment's cycle of birth and death
To fullness of eternal life in me.

Still your mind in me, still yourself in me,
And without doubt you shall be united with me,
Lord of Love, dwelling in your heart.
But if you cannot still your mind in me,
Learn to do so through the practice of meditation.
If you lack the will for such self-discipline,
Engage yourself in selfless service of all around you,
For selfless service can lead you at last to me.
If you are unable to do even this,
Surrender yourself to me in love,
Receiving success and failure with equal calmness
As granted by me.

Better indeed is knowledge than mechanical practice.
Better than knowledge is meditation.
But better still is surrender in love,
Because there follows immediate peace.

That one I love who is incapable of ill will,
And returns love for hatred.
Living beyond the reach of *I* and *mine*
And of pleasure and pain, full of mercy,
Contented, self-controlled, firm in faith,
With all their heart and all their mind given to me –
With such people I am in love.

Not agitating the world or by it agitated,
They stand above the sway of elation,
Competition, and fear, accepting life
Good and bad as it comes. They are pure,
Efficient, detached, ready to meet every demand
I make on them as a humble instrument of my work.

They are dear to me who run not after the pleasant
Or away from the painful, grieve not
Over the past, lust not today,
But let things come and go as they happen.

Who serve both friend and foe with equal love,
Not buoyed up by praise or cast down by blame,
Alike in heat and cold, pleasure and pain,
Free from selfish attachments and self-will,
Ever full, in harmony everywhere,
Firm in faith – such as these are dear to me.

But dearest to me are those who seek me
In faith and love as life's eternal goal.
They go beyond death to immortality.

Beloved of the Soul

Beloved of the soul, source of compassion,
Shape your servant to your will.
Then your servant will run like a deer to bow before you.
Your love will be sweeter than a honeycomb.
Majestic, beautiful, light of the universe,
My soul is lovesick for you;
I implore you, God, heal her
By revealing to her your pleasant radiance;
Then she will be strengthened and healed
And will have eternal joy.
Timeless One, be compassionate
And have mercy on the one you love,
For this is my deepest desire:
To see your magnificent splendor.
This is what my heart longs for;
Have mercy and do not conceal yourself.
Reveal yourself, my Beloved,
And spread the shelter of your peace over me;
Light up the world with your glory;
We will celebrate you in joy.
Hurry, Beloved, the time has come,
And grant us grace, as in days of old.

The Inner Ruler

The Lord is enshrined in the hearts of all.
The Lord is the supreme reality.
Rejoice in him through renunciation.
Covet nothing. All belongs to the Lord.
Thus working may you live a hundred years.
Thus alone can you work in full freedom.

Those who deny the Self are born again
Blind to the Self, enveloped in darkness,
Utterly devoid of love for the Lord.

The Self is one. Ever still, the Self is
Swifter than thought, swifter than the senses.
Though motionless, he outruns all pursuit.
Without the Self, never could life exist.

The Self seems to move, but is ever still.
He seems far away, but is ever near.
He is within all, and he transcends all.

Those who see all creatures in themselves
And themselves in all creatures know no fear.
Those who see all creatures in themselves
And themselves in all creatures know no grief.
How can the multiplicity of life
Delude the one who sees its unity?

The Self is everywhere. Bright is the Self,
Indivisible, untouched by sin, wise,
Immanent and transcendent. He it is
Who holds the cosmos together.

In dark night live those
For whom the world without alone is real;
In night darker still, for whom the world within
Alone is real. The first leads to a life
Of action, the second of meditation.
But those who combine action with meditation
Go across the sea of death through action
And enter into immortality
Through the practice of meditation.
So have we heard from the wise.

In dark night live those for whom the Lord
Is transcendent only; in night darker still,
For whom he is immanent only.
But those for whom he is transcendent
And immanent cross the sea of death
With the immanent and enter into
Immortality with the transcendent.
So have we heard from the wise.

The face of truth is hidden by your orb
Of gold, O sun. May you remove the orb
So that I, who adore the true, may see
The glory of truth. O nourishing sun,
Solitary traveler, controller,
Source of life for all creatures, spread your light,
And subdue your dazzling splendor
So that I may see your blessed Self.
Even that very Self am I!

May my life merge in the Immortal
When my body is reduced to ashes!
O mind, meditate on the eternal
Brahman. Remember the deeds of the past.
Remember, O mind, remember.

O God of fire, lead us by the good path
To eternal joy. You know all our deeds.
Deliver us from evil, we that bow
And pray again and again.

O M *Shanti Shanti Shanti*

The Earth Is the Lord's

The earth is the Lord's,
    and the fullness thereof;
the world, and they that dwell therein.
For he hath founded it upon the seas,
    and established it upon the floods.

Who shall ascend into the hill of the Lord?
    or who shall stand in his holy place?
He that hath clean hands and a pure heart;
    who hath not lifted up his soul unto vanity,
    nor sworn deceitfully.
He shall receive the blessing from the Lord,
    and righteousness from the God of his salvation.
This is the generation of them that seek him,
    that seek thy face, O Jacob.   *Selah*
Lift up your heads, O ye gates;
    and be ye lift up, ye everlasting doors;
    and the King of glory shall come in.
Who is this King of glory? The Lord strong and mighty,
    the Lord mighty in battle.
Lift up your heads, O ye gates;
    even lift them up, ye everlasting doors;
    and the King of glory shall come in.
Who is this King of glory? The Lord of hosts,
    he is the King of glory.   *Selah*

Serve the Lord with Gladness

Make a joyful noise unto the Lord,
    all ye lands.
Serve the Lord with gladness:
    come before his presence with singing.
Know ye that the Lord he is God:
    it is he that hath made us,
    and not we ourselves;
We are his people,
    and the sheep of his pasture.

Enter into his gates with thanksgiving,
    and into his courts with praise:
Be thankful unto him,
    and bless his name.
For the Lord is good;
    his mercy is everlasting;
And his truth endureth
    to all generations.

The Sermon on the Mount

1

Blessed are the poor in spirit:
    for theirs is the kingdom of heaven.

Blessed are they that mourn:
    for they shall be comforted.

Blessed are the meek:
    for they shall inherit the earth.

Blessed are they which do hunger and thirst
    after righteousness:
    for they shall be filled.

Blessed are the merciful:
    for they shall obtain mercy.

Blessed are the pure in heart:
    for they shall see God.

Blessed are the peacemakers:
    for they shall be called the children of God.

Blessed are they which are persecuted
    for righteousness' sake:
    for theirs is the kingdom of heaven.

Blessed are ye, when men shall revile you, and persecute you, and shall say all manner of evil against you falsely, for my sake. Rejoice, and be exceeding glad: for great is your reward in heaven: for so persecuted they the prophets which were before you.

Ye are the salt of the earth: but if the salt have lost his savor, wherewith shall it be salted? It is thenceforth good for nothing, but to be cast out, and to be trodden under foot of men.

Ye are the light of the world. A city that is set on an hill cannot be hid. Neither do men light a candle, and put it under a bushel, but on a candlestick; and it giveth light unto all that are in the house. Let your light so shine before men, that they may see your good works, and glorify your Father which is in heaven.

2

Ye have heard that it hath been said,
Thou shalt love thy neighbor, and hate thine enemy.
But I say unto you,

Love your enemies, bless them that curse you, do good to them that hate you, and pray for them which despitefully use you, and persecute you; that ye may be the children of your Father which is in heaven: for he maketh his sun to rise on the evil and on the good, and sendeth rain on the just and on the unjust.

For if ye love them which love you, what reward have ye? Do not even the publicans the same?
And if ye salute your brethren only, what do ye more than others? Do not even the publicans so?

Be ye therefore perfect,
even as your Father which is in heaven is perfect.

The Sermon on the Mount

3

Our Father which art in heaven, hallowed be thy name.
Thy kingdom come,
Thy will be done in earth, as it is in heaven.
Give us this day our daily bread,
And forgive us our debts, as we forgive our debtors.
And lead us not into temptation, but deliver us from evil:
For thine is the kingdom,
     and the power, and the glory, for ever.   *Amen*

Part Three

Songs of Sri Ramakrishna

1

Dwell, O mind, within yourself;
Enter no other's home.
If you but seek there, you will find
All you are searching for.
God, the true Philosopher's Stone,
Who answers every prayer,
Lies hidden deep within your heart,
The richest gem of all.
How many pearls and precious stones
Are scattered all about
The outer court that lies before
The chamber of your heart!

Oh, when will dawn for me that day of blessedness
When he who is all Good, all Beauty, and all Truth
Will light the inmost shrine of my heart?
When shall I sink at last, ever beholding him,
Into that Ocean of Delight?
Lord, as Infinite Wisdom thou shalt enter my soul,
And my unquiet mind, made speechless by thy sight,
Will find a haven at thy feet.
In my heart's firmament, O Lord, thou wilt arise
As Blissful Immortality; and as, when the chakora
Beholds the rising moon, it sports about for very joy,
So, too, shall I be filled with heavenly happiness
When thou appearest unto me.

Thou One without a Second, all Peace,
    the King of Kings!
At thy beloved feet I shall renounce my life
And so at last shall gain life's goal;
I shall enjoy the bliss of heaven while yet on earth!
Where else is a boon so rare bestowed?
Then shall I see thy Glory, pure and untouched by stain;
As darkness flees from light, so will my darkest sins
Desert me at thy dawn's approach. Kindle in me, O Lord,
The blazing fire of faith to be the pole-star of my life;
O Succour of the weak, fulfill my one desire!
Then shall I bathe both day and night
In the boundless bliss of thy Love, and utterly forget
Myself, O Lord, attaining thee.

3

I have joined my heart to thee:
    all that exists art thou;
Thee only have I found, for thou art all that exists.
O Lord, Beloved of my heart!
    Thou art the Home of all;
Where, indeed, is the heart in which thou dost not dwell?
Thou hast entered every heart:
    all that exists art thou.
Whether sage or fool, whether Hindu or Mussalman,
Thou makest them as thou wilt:
    all that exists art thou.
Thy presence is everywhere,
    whether in heaven or in Kaaba;
Before thee all must bow, for thou art all that exists.
From earth below to the highest heaven,
    from heaven to deepest earth,
I see thee wherever I look: all that exists art thou.
Pondering, I have understood;
    I have seen it beyond a doubt;
I find not a single thing that may be compared to thee.
To Jafar it has been revealed
    that thou art all that exists.

Believing in Mind

The great Way has no impediments;
It does not pick and choose.
When you abandon attachment and aversion
You see it plainly.
Make a thousandth of an inch distinction,
Heaven and earth swing apart.
If you want it to appear before your eyes,
Cherish neither *for* nor *against*.

To compare what you like with what you dislike,
That is the disease of the mind.
You pass over the hidden meaning;
Peace of mind is needlessly troubled.

It is round and perfect like vast space,
Lacks nothing, never overflows.
Only because we take and reject
Do we lose the means to know its Suchness.

Don't get tangled in outward desire
Or get caught within yourself.
Once you plant deep the longing for peace
Confusion leaves of itself.

Return to the root and find meaning;
Follow sense objects, you lose the goal.
Just one instant of inner enlightenment
Will take you far beyond the emptiness of the world.

Selfish attachment forgets all limits;
It always leads down evil roads.
When you let go of it, things happen of themselves;
The substance neither goes nor abides.

If the eye does not sleep
All dreams will naturally stop.
If the mind does not differentiate
All things are of one Suchness.

When you fathom the realm of Suchness
You instantly forget all selfish desire.
Having seen ten thousand things as one
You return to your natural state.

Without meditation
Consciousness and feeling are hard to grasp.
In the realm of Suchness
There is neither self nor other.

In the one, there is the all.
In the all, there is the one.
If you know this,
You will never worry about being incomplete.

If belief and mind are made the same
And there is no division between belief and mind
The road of words comes to an end,
Beyond present and future.

The Hidden Self

The mind may be said to be of two kinds,
Pure and impure. Driven by the senses
It becomes impure; but with the senses
Under control, the mind becomes pure.

It is the mind that frees us or enslaves.
Driven by the senses we become bound;
Master of the senses we become free.
Those who seek freedom must master their senses.

When the mind is detached from the senses
One reaches the summit of consciousness.
Mastery of the mind leads to wisdom.
Practice meditation. Stop all vain talk.
The highest state is beyond reach of thought,
For it lies beyond all duality.

Keep repeating the ancient mantram O M
Until it reverberates in your heart.

Brahman is indivisible and pure;
Realize Brahman and go beyond all change.
He is immanent and transcendent.
Realizing him, sages attain freedom
And declare there are no separate minds.
They have but realized what they always are.

Waking, sleeping, dreaming, the Self is one.
Transcend these three and go beyond rebirth.

There is only one Self in all creatures.
The One appears many, just as the moon
Appears many, reflected in water.

The Self appears to change its location
But does not, just as air in a jar
Changes not when the jar is moved about.
When the jar is broken, the air knows not;
But the Self knows well when the body is shed.

We see not the Self, concealed by maya;
When the veil falls, we see we are the Self.

The mantram is the symbol of Brahman;
Repeating it can bring peace to the mind.

Knowledge is twofold, lower and higher.
Realize the Self; for all else is lower.
Realization is rice; all else is chaff.

The milk of cows of any hue is white.
The sages say that wisdom is the milk
And the sacred scriptures are the cows.

As butter lies hidden within milk,
The Self is hidden in the hearts of all.
Churn the mind through meditation on it;
Light your fire through meditation on it:
The Self, all whole, all peace, all certitude.

"I have realized the Self," declares the sage,
"Who is present in all beings.
I am united with the Lord of Love;
I am united with the Lord of Love."

O M *Shanti Shanti Shanti*

The Hidden Self
99

The Lamp of Wisdom

To all who long and strive to realize the Self,
Illumination comes to them in this very life.
This divine awareness never leaves them,
And they work unceasingly for the good of all.
When the lamp of wisdom is lit within,
Their face shines, whether life brings weal or woe.
Even in deep sleep they are aware of the Self,
For their mind is freed from all conditioning.
Inwardly they are pure like the cloudless sky,
But they act as if they too were like us all.
Free from self-will, with detached intellect,
They are aware of the Self even with their hands at work.
Neither afraid of the world, nor making the world afraid,
They are free from greed, anger, and fear.

When the waves of self-will subside
Into the sea of peace that is the Self,
The mind becomes still, the heart pure,
And illumination comes to us in this very life.
When this supreme state is attained,
They neither rise nor fall, change nor die.
Words cannot describe the supreme state
For it is fuller than fullness can be.

Shine Through Us

Dear Jesus, help us to spread your fragrance
    everywhere we go.
Flood our souls with your spirit and life.
Penetrate and possess our whole being so utterly
    that our lives may only be a radiance of yours.
Shine through us, and be so in us,
    that every soul we come in contact with
    may feel your presence in our soul.
Let them look up and see no longer us
    but only Jesus!
Stay with us, and then we shall begin to shine
    as you shine; so to shine as to be a light to others;
    the light, O Jesus, will be all from you,
    none of it will be ours;
    it will be you, shining on others through us.
Let us thus praise you in the way you love best
    by shining on those around us.
Let us preach you without preaching, not by words
    but by our example, by the catching force,
    the sympathetic influence of what we do,
    the evident fullness of the love
    our hearts bear to you.   *Amen.*

The Shining Self

Let us meditate on the shining Self,
Changeless, underlying the world of change,
And realized in the heart in samadhi.

Hard to reach is the supreme goal of life,
Hard to describe and hard to abide in.
They alone attain samadhi who have
Mastered their senses and are free from anger,
Free from self-will and from likes and dislikes,
Without selfish bonds to people and things.

They alone attain samadhi who are
Prepared to face challenge after challenge
In the three stages of meditation.
Under an illumined teacher's guidance
They become united with the Lord of Love,
Called Vishnu, who is present everywhere.
Though the three gunas emanate from him,
He is infinite and invisible.
Though all the galaxies emerge from him,
He is without form and unconditioned.

To be united with the Lord of Love
Is to be freed from all conditioning.
This is the state of Self-realization,
Far beyond the reach of words and thoughts.
To be united with the Lord of Love,
Imperishable, changeless, beyond cause
And effect, is to find infinite joy.

Brahman is beyond all duality,
Beyond the reach of thinker and of thought.

Let us meditate on the shining Self,
The ultimate reality, who is
Realized by the sages in samadhi.

Brahman cannot be realized by those
Who are subject to greed, fear, and anger.
Brahman cannot be realized by those
Who are subject to the pride of name and fame
Or to the vanity of scholarship.
Brahman cannot be realized by those
Who are enmeshed in life's duality.

But to all those who pierce this duality,
Whose hearts are given to the Lord of Love,
He gives himself through his infinite grace;
He gives himself through his infinite grace.

O M *Shanti Shanti Shanti*

Whatever You Do

A leaf, a flower, a fruit, or even
Water, offered to me in devotion,
I will accept as the loving gift
Of a dedicated heart. Whatever you do,
Make it an offering to me –
The food you eat or worship you perform,
The help you give, even your suffering.
Thus will you be free from karma's bondage,
From the results of action, good and bad.

I am the same to all beings. My love
Is the same always. Nevertheless, those
Who meditate on me with devotion,
They dwell in me, and I shine forth in them.

Even the worst sinner becomes a saint
When he loves me with all his heart. This love
Will soon transform his personality
And fill his heart with peace profound.
O son of Kunti, this is my promise:
Those who love me, they shall never perish.

Even those who are handicapped by birth
Have reached the supreme goal in life
By taking refuge in me. How much more
The pure brahmins and royal sages who love me!

Give not your love to this transient world
Of suffering, but give all your love to me.
Give me your mind, your heart, all your worship.
Long for me always, live for me always,
And you shall be united with me.

Teach Me

Be it mine to look up to thy light, even from afar, even from the depths. Teach me to seek thee, and reveal thyself to me when I seek thee, for I cannot seek thee except thou teach me, nor find thee, except thou reveal thyself. Let me seek thee in longing, let me long for thee in seeking; let me find thee in love, and love thee in finding.

Lord, I acknowledge and I thank thee that thou hast created me in this thine image, in order that I may be mindful of thee, may conceive of thee, and love thee; but that image has been so consumed and wasted away by vices, and obscured by the smoke of wrong-doing, that it cannot achieve that for which it was made, except thou renew it, and create it anew.

I do not endeavor, O Lord, to penetrate thy sublimity, for in no wise do I compare my understanding with that; but I long to understand in some degree thy truth, which my heart believes and loves. For I do not seek to understand that I may believe, but I believe in order to understand. For this also I believe: that unless I believed I should not understand.

TUKARAM

The One Thing Needed

Of what avail this restless, hurrying activity?
This heavy weight of earthly duties?
God's purposes stand firm,
And thou, his little one,
Needest one thing alone:
Trust in his power, and will, to meet thy need.
Thy burden resteth safe on him,
And thou, his little one,
Mayst play securely at his side.
This is the sum and substance of it all:
God is,
God loveth thee,
God beareth all thy care.

The Blessing of a Well-Trained Mind

As an archer aims his arrow, the wise aim their restless thoughts, hard to aim, hard to restrain.

As a fish hooked and left on the sand thrashes about in agony, the mind being trained in meditation trembles all over, desperate to escape the hand of Mara.

Hard it is to train the mind, which goes where it likes and does what it wants. But a trained mind brings health and happiness. The wise can direct their thoughts, subtle and elusive, wherever they choose: a trained mind brings health and happiness.

Those who can direct thoughts, which are unsubstantial and wander so aimlessly, are freed from the bonds of Mara.

They are not wise whose thoughts are not steady and minds not serene, who do not know dharma, the law of life. They are wise whose thoughts are steady and minds serene, unaffected by good and bad. They are awake and free from fear.

Remember, this body is like a fragile clay pot. Make your mind a fortress and conquer Mara with the weapon of wisdom. Guard your conquest always.

Remember that this body will soon lie in the earth without life, without value, useless as a burned log.

More than those who hate you, more than all your enemies, an untrained mind does greater harm. More than your mother, more than your father, more than all your family, a well-trained mind does greater good.

Duties of the Heart

What is meant by wholehearted devotion to God alone? It means that in every act, public and private, the aim and purpose should be purely work for God's sake, to please him only, without winning the approval of other people. How achieve wholehearted devotion to God alone? In ten ways. If these are firmly set in your heart and you clearly make them the basis of your actions, then your devotion to God will be complete. Then you will turn to no one else, set your hope on nothing else, and mold your will to none other than God's.

First is wholehearted acceptance that only God fills the universe;

second, that God is the source of all reality and is endlessly good;

third, that your goal is to work for God;

fourth, that you should rely on God alone and not physical beings;

fifth, that you get no ultimate gain or loss from physical beings, but only from the Creator;

sixth, that you should maintain evenness of mind regardless of whether people praise you or blame you;

seventh, that you should not make a show of spiritual activities to impress other people;

eighth, that you should not be caught up in personal gain when you are working for eternal life;

ninth, that you should hold God in reverence and be humble before him;

tenth, that you should use your mind to master your senses and use them with care and discrimination.

The Unstruck Bells and Drums

The Lord is in me, the Lord is in you,
    as life is in every seed.
O servant! Put false pride away, and seek for him
    within you.
A million suns are ablaze with light,
The sea of blue spreads in the sky,
The fever of life is stilled, and all stains
    are washed away
When I sit in the midst of that world.

Hark to the unstruck bells and drums!
Take your delight in love!
Rains pour down without water, and the rivers
    are streams of light.
One love it is that pervades the whole world,
    few there are who know it fully:
They are blind who hope to see it by the light of reason,
    that reason which is the cause of separation –
The house of reason is very far away!

How blessed is Kabir, that amidst this great joy he sings
    within his own vessel.
It is the music of the meeting of soul with soul;
It is the music of the forgetting of sorrows;
It is the music that transcends all coming in
    and all going forth.

Just Because You Are My God

Oh, my God, I want to love you
Not that I might gain eternal heaven
Nor escape eternal hell
But, Lord, to love you just because
    you are my God.

Grant me to give to you
And not to count the cost,
To fight for you
And not to mind the wounds,
To labor and to ask for no reward
    except the knowledge that I
    serve my God.

You Are Christ's Hands

Christ has no body now on earth but yours,
    no hands but yours,
    no feet but yours,
Yours are the eyes through which is to look out
    Christ's compassion to the world;
Yours are the feet with which he is to go about
    doing good;
Yours are the hands with which he is to bless men now.

The Path

I know the path: it is strait and narrow.
It is like the edge of a sword. I rejoice to
walk on it. I weep when I slip. God's word is:
"He who strives never perishes."
I have implicit faith in that promise. Though,
therefore, from my weakness I fail a thousand times,
I shall not lose faith.

Be Aware of Me Always

SRI KRISHNA:
Those who are free from selfish attachments,
Who have mastered the senses and passions,
Act not, but are acted through by the Lord.
Listen to me now, O son of Kunti,
How one who has become an instrument
In the hands of the Lord attains Brahman,
The supreme consummation of wisdom.

Unerring in discrimination,
Sovereign of the senses and passions,
Free from the clamor of likes and dislikes,
They lead a simple, self-reliant life
Based on meditation, using speech,
Body, and mind to serve the Lord of Love.

Free from self-will, aggressiveness, arrogance,
From the lust to possess people or things,
They are at peace with themselves and others
And enter into the unitive state.

United with the Lord, ever joyful,
Beyond the reach of self-will and sorrow,
They serve me in every living creature
And attain supreme devotion to me.
By loving me they share in my glory
And enter into my boundless being.

All their acts are performed in my service,
And through my grace they win eternal life.

Make every act an offering to me;
Regard me as your only protector.
Make every thought an offering to me;
Meditate on me always.

Drawing upon your deepest resources,
You shall overcome all difficulties
Through my grace. But if you will not heed me
In your self-will, nothing will avail you.

If you say, "I will not fight this battle,"
Your own nature will drive you into it.
If you will not fight the battle of life,
Your own karma will drive you into it.

The Lord dwells in the hearts of all creatures,
And he whirls them round on the wheel of time.
Run to him for refuge with all your strength
And peace profound will be yours through his grace.

I give you these precious words of wisdom;
Reflect on them and then choose what is best.
These are the last words I shall speak to you,
Dear one, for your spiritual fulfillment.

Be aware of me always, adore me,
Make every act an offering to me,
And you shall come to me;
This I promise, for you are dear to me.
Leave all other support, and look to me
For protection. I shall purify you
From the sins of the past. Do not grieve.

Do not share this wisdom with anyone
Who lacks in devotion or self-control,
Lacks the desire to learn, or who scoffs at me.

Those who teach this supreme mystery
Of the Gita to all those who love me
Will come to me without doubt. No one
Can render me more devoted service;
No one on earth can be more dear to me.

Those who meditate on these holy words
Worship me with wisdom and devotion.
Even those who listen to them with faith,
Free from doubts, will find a happier world.

Have you fully understood my message?
Are you free from your doubts and delusions?

ARJUNA:
You have dispelled my doubts and delusions
And made me ready to fight this battle.
My faith is firm now, and I will do your will.

Part Four

Radiant Is the World Soul

Radiant is the world soul,
Full of splendor and beauty,
Full of life,
Of souls hidden,
Of treasures of the holy spirit,
Of fountains of strength,
Of greatness and beauty.
Proudly I ascend
Toward the heights of the world soul
That gives life to the universe.
How majestic the vision – Come, enjoy,
Come, find peace,
Embrace delight,
Taste and see that God is good.
Why spend your substance on what does not nourish
And your labor on what cannot satisfy?
Listen to me, and you will enjoy what is good,
And find delight in what is truly precious.

Lord That Giveth Strength

1

My child, I am the Lord, that giveth strength in the day of tribulation.

Come thou unto me, when it is not well with thee.

This is that which most of all hindereth heavenly consolation, that thou art too slow in turning thyself unto prayer.

For before thou dost earnestly supplicate me, thou seekest in the meanwhile many comforts, and refreshest thyself in outward things.

And hence it comes to pass that all doth little profit thee, until thou well consider that I am he who do rescue them that trust in me; and that out of me, there is neither powerful help, nor profitable counsel, nor lasting remedy.

But do thou, having now recovered breath after the tempest, gather strength again in the light of my mercies; for I am at hand (saith the Lord) to repair all, not only entirely, but also abundantly and in most plentiful measure.

2

Is there anything hard to me? or shall I be like one that saith and doeth not?

Where is thy faith? stand firmly and with perseverance; take courage and be patient; comfort will come to thee in due time.

Wait, wait, I say, for me: I will come and take care of thee.

It is a temptation that vexeth thee, and a vain fear that affrighteth thee.

What else doth anxiety about future contingencies bring thee, but sorrow upon sorrow? *Sufficient for the day is the evil thereof.*

It is a vain thing and unprofitable, to be either disturbed or pleased about future things, which perhaps will never come to pass.

3

But it is incident to man, to be deluded with such imaginations; and a sign of a mind as yet weak, to be so easily drawn away by the suggestions of the Enemy.

For so he may delude and deceive thee, he careth not whether it be by true or by false propositions; nor whether he overthrows thee with the love of present, or the fear of future things.

Let not therefore thy heart be troubled, neither let it fear. Trust in me, and put thy confidence in my mercy.

When thou thinkest thyself farthest off from me, often-times I am nearest unto thee.

When thou countest almost all to be lost, then oftentimes the greatest gain of reward is close at hand.

All is not lost, when any thing falleth out contrary.

Thou oughtest not to judge according to present feeling; nor so to take any grief, or give thyself over to it, from whencesoever it cometh, as though all hopes of escape were quite taken away.

4

Think not thyself wholly left, although for a time I have sent thee some tribulation, or even have withdrawn thy desired comfort; for this is the way to the kingdom of heaven.

And without doubt it is more expedient for thee and the rest of my servants, that ye be exercised with adversities, than that ye should have all things according to your desires.

I know the secret thoughts of thy heart, and that it is very expedient for thy welfare, that thou be left sometimes without taste (of spiritual sweetness, and in a dry condi-tion), lest perhaps thou shouldest be puffed up with thy prosperous estate, and shouldest be willing to please thyself in that which thou art not.

That which I have given, I can take away; and I can restore it again when I please.

5

When I give it, it is mine; when I withdraw it, I take
not any thing that is thine; for mine is every good gift
and every perfect gift.

If I send upon thee affliction, or any cross whatever,
repine not, nor let thy heart fail thee; I can quickly
succor thee, and turn all thy heaviness into joy.

Howbeit I am righteous, and greatly to be praised when
I deal thus with thee.

6

If thou art wise, and considerest what the truth is, thou
never oughtest to mourn dejectedly for any adversity that
befalleth thee, but rather to rejoice and give thanks.

Yea, thou wilt account this time especial joy, that I afflict
thee with sorrows, and do not spare thee.

As the Father hath loved me, I also love you, said I unto my
beloved disciples; whom certainly I sent not out to temporal joys, but to great conflicts; not to honors, but to
contempts; not to idleness, but to labors; not to rest, but
to bring forth much fruit with patience. Remember thou
these words, O my child!

The Fruit of the Tree

No longer am I
The man I used to be;
For I have plucked the fruit
Of this precious tree of life.

As the river flows down the hills
And becomes one with the sea,
So has this weaver's love flowed
To become one with the Lord of Love.

Go deeper and deeper in meditation
To reach the seabed of consciousness.
Through the blessing of my teacher
I have passed beyond the land of death.

Says Kabir: Listen to me, friends,
And cast away all your doubts.
Make your faith unshakable in the Lord,
And pass beyond the land of death.

Weaving Your Name

I weave your name on the loom of my mind,
To make my garment when you come to me.
My loom has ten thousand threads
To make my garment when you come to me.
The sun and moon watch while I weave your name;
The sun and moon hear while I count your name.
These are the wages I get by day and night
To deposit in the lotus bank of my heart.

I weave your name on the loom of my mind
To clean and soften ten thousand threads
And to comb the twists and knots of my thoughts.
No more shall I weave a garment of pain.
For you have come to me, drawn by my weaving,
Ceaselessly weaving your name on the loom of my mind.

Forgiveness

The child makes many a mistake,
But the mother forgives them all.
I am your child, your wayward child,
Lord, won't you forgive my sins?

If the child throws a temper tantrum
And pulls and pushes his mother,
She does not move away from him
Nor pull and push in return.
I am your child, your wayward child,
Lord, won't you forgive my sins?

My mind is trapped in depression;
How can I free my mind without your name?
I am your child, your wayward child,
Lord, won't you forgive my sins?

Bless me with a loving heart and a peaceful mind,
And draw me into full absorption in you.
I am your child, your wayward child,
Lord, won't you forgive my sins?

The River of God

Spiritual aspirants ask their teacher:
What is the cause of the cosmos? Is it Brahman?
From where do we come? By what live?
Where shall we find peace at last?
What power governs the duality
Of pleasure and pain by which we are driven?

Time, nature, necessity, accident,
Elements, energy, intelligence –
None of these can be the first Cause.
They are effects, whose only purpose is
To help the self to rise above pleasure and pain.

In the depths of meditation, sages
Saw within themselves the Lord of Love,
Who dwells in the heart of every creature.
Deep in the hearts of all he dwells, hidden
Behind the gunas of law, energy,
And inertia. He is One. He it is
Who rules over time, space, and causality.

The world is the wheel of God, turning round
And round with all living creatures upon
The wheel. The world is the river of God,
Flowing from him and flowing back to him.

On this ever-revolving wheel of life
The individual self goes round and round
Through life after life, believing itself

To be a separate creature, until
It sees its identity with the Lord
Of Love and attains immortality
In the indivisible Whole.

He is the eternal reality, sing
The scriptures, and the ground of existence.
They who perceive him in every creature
Merge in him and are released from the wheel
Of birth and death.

The Lord of Love holds in his hand the world,
Composed of the changing and the changeless,
The manifest and the unmanifest.
The individual self, not yet aware
Of the Lord, goes after pleasure, to become
Bound more and more. When it sees the Lord,
There comes the end of its bondage.

Conscious spirit and unconscious matter
Both have existed since the dawn of time,
With maya appearing to connect them,
Misrepresenting joy as eternal.
When all these three are seen as one, the Self
Reveals its universal form and serves
As an instrument of the divine will.

All is change in the world of the senses,
But changeless is the supreme Lord of Love.
Meditate on him, be absorbed in him,
Wake up from this dream of separateness.

Know God and all fetters will fall away.
No longer identifying yourself
With the body, go beyond birth and death.
All your desires will be fulfilled in him
Who is One without a second.

Know him to be enshrined within your heart
Always. Truly there is nothing more
To know in life. Meditate and realize
The world is filled with the presence of God.

Fire is not seen until one firestick rubs
Against another, though the fire remains
Hidden in the firestick. So does the Lord
Remain hidden in the body until
He is revealed through the mystic mantram.

Let your body be the lower firestick;
Let the mantram be the upper. Rub them
Against each other in meditation
And realize the Lord.

Like oil in sesame seeds, like butter
In cream, like water in springs, like fire
In a firestick, so dwells the Lord of Love,
The Self, in the very depths of consciousness.
Realize him through truth and meditation.

The Self is hidden in the hearts of all,
As butter lies hidden in cream. Realize
The Self in the depths of meditation,
The Lord of Love, supreme reality,
Who is the goal of all knowledge.

This is the highest mystical teaching;
This is the highest mystical teaching.

LAO TZU

The Best

The best, like water,
Benefit all and do not compete.
They dwell in lowly spots that everyone else scorns.
Putting others before themselves,
They find themselves in the foremost place
And come very near to the Tao.
In their dwelling, they love the earth;
In their heart, they love what is deep;
In personal relationships, they love kindness;
In their words, they love truth.
In the world, they love peace.
In personal affairs, they love what is right.
In action, they love choosing the right time.
It is because they do not compete with others
That they are beyond the reproach of the world.

The Path to Your Dwelling

How am I to come to you,
When I stand outside a locked gate?
The path to your dwelling
Runs steep and dangerous.
In fear I climb, step by step,
The path to your dwelling,
So steep and dangerous.
O Lord, you seem so far away
That my mind goes up and down.
As I climb, the sentinels watch
And the robbers wait to waylay me.
Though the path to your dwelling
Is steep and dangerous,
You have called me home.
Meera's wanderings are ended.
She has found her way to your feet.

Come, Beloved

As the lotus dies without water,
As the night is blind without the moon,
So is my heart without you, Beloved.
I wander alone at night,
Driven by my longing for you.
I hunger for you all the day,
I thirst for you all the night.
My grief is beyond words
My mind is beyond rest.
Come and end my grief, Beloved.
Come and bring joy to my heart.
You know my inmost secret;
Then look at me with eyes of love,
Your slave for countless lives
    since the dawn of time.
So says Meera at your feet.

Life of My Life

You are the life of my life,
O Krishna, the heart of my heart.
There is none in all the three worlds
Whom I call my own but you.

You are the peace of my mind;
You are the joy of my heart;
You are my beauty and my wealth.

You are my wisdom and my strength;
I call you my home, my friend, my kin.

My present and future are in your hands;
My scriptures and commands come from you.
Supreme teacher, fountain of wisdom,
You are the path and the goal,
Tender mother and stern father too.

You are the creator and protector,
And the pilot who takes me across
The stormy ocean of life.

Christ Be With Me

May the strength of God pilot me,
the power of God preserve me today.

May the wisdom of God instruct me,
the eye of God watch over me,
the ear of God hear me,
the word of God give me sweet talk,
the hand of God defend me,
the way of God guide me.

Christ be with me.
Christ before me.
Christ after me.
Christ in me.
Christ under me.
Christ over me.
Christ on my right hand.
Christ on my left hand.
Christ on this side.
Christ on that side.
Christ at my back.

Christ in the head of everyone
to whom I speak.
Christ in the mouth of every person
who speaks to me.

Christ in the eye of every person
who looks at me.
Christ in the ear of every person
who hears me today.

The Self

The student inquires: "Who makes my mind think?
Who fills my body with vitality?
Who causes my tongue to speak? Who is that
Invisible One who sees through my eyes
And hears through my ears?"

The teacher replies: "The Self is the ear of the ear,
The eye of the eye, the mind of the mind,
The word of words, and the life of life.
Rising above the senses and the mind
And renouncing separate existence,
The wise realize the deathless Self.

"Him our eyes cannot see, nor words express;
He cannot be grasped even by our mind.
We do not know, we cannot understand,
Because he is different from the known
And he is different from the unknown.
Thus have we heard from the illumined ones.

"That which makes the tongue speak, but cannot be
Spoken by the tongue, know that as the Self.
This Self is not someone other than you.

"That which makes the mind think, but cannot be
Thought by the mind, that is the Self indeed.
This Self is not someone other than you.

"That which makes the eye see, but cannot be
Seen by the eye, that is the Self indeed.
This Self is not someone other than you.

"That which makes the ear hear, but cannot be
Heard by the ear, that is the Self indeed.
This Self is not someone other than you.

"That which makes you draw breath, but cannot be
Drawn by your breath, that is the Self indeed.
This Self is not someone other than you."

The Brahmin

Cross the river bravely,
Conquer all your passions,
Go beyond the world of fragments,
And know the deathless ground of life.

Cross the river bravely,
Conquer all your passions,
Go beyond your likes and dislikes
And all fetters will fall away.

Who is a true brahmin?
Him I call a brahmin
Who has neither likes nor dislikes,
And is free from the chains of fear.

Who is a true brahmin?
Him I call a brahmin
Who has trained his mind to be still
And reached the supreme goal of life.

The sun shines in the day;
In the night, the moon;
The warrior shines in battle;
In meditation, the brahmin.
But day and night the Buddha shines
In radiance of love for all.

Him I call a brahmin
Who has shed all evil.

He is called *samana,* "the serene,"
And *pabbajita,* "a pure one."

Him I call a brahmin
Who is never angry,
Never causes harm to others
Even when he is harmed by them.

Him I call a brahmin
Who clings not to pleasure.
Do not cause sorrow to others:
No more sorrow will come to you.

Him I call a brahmin
Who does not hurt others
With unkind acts, words, or thoughts.
His body and mind obey him.

Him I call a brahmin
Who walks in the footsteps
Of the Buddha. Light your torch too
From the fire of his sacrifice.

Not matted hair nor birth
Makes a man a brahmin,
But the truth and love for all life
With which his heart is full.

Of what use is matted hair?
Of what use a skin of deer
On which to sit in meditation,
If your mind is seething with lust?

Saffron robe, outward show,
Does not make a brahmin,
But training of the mind and senses
Through practice of meditation.

The Brahmin
141

Not riches nor high caste
Makes a man a brahmin.
Free yourself from selfish desires
And you will become a brahmin.

He has thrown off his chains;
He trembles not in fear.
No selfish bonds can ensnare him,
No impure thought pollute his mind.

Him I call a brahmin
Who fears not jail nor death.
He has the power of love
No army can defeat.

Him I call a brahmin
Who clings not to pleasure,
Like water on a lotus leaf,
Or mustard seed on a needle.

Him I call a brahmin
Ever true, ever kind.
He never asks what life can give,
But "What can I give life?"

Him I call a brahmin
Who has found his heaven,
Free from every selfish desire,
Free from every impurity.

For him no more sorrow will come.
On him no more burden will fall.

Him I call a brahmin
Who has risen above
The duality of this world,
Free from sorrow and free from sin.

He shines like the full moon
With no cloud in the sky.

Him I call a brahmin
Who has crossed the river,
Difficult, dangerous to cross,
And safely reached the other shore.

Wanting nothing at all,
Doubting nothing at all,
Master of his body and mind,
He has gone beyond time and death.

Him I call a brahmin
Who turns his back on himself.
Homeless, he is ever at home;
Egoless, he is ever full.

Him I call a brahmin
Who is free from bondage
To human beings and nature,
The hero who has conquered the world.

Self-will has left his mind;
It will never return.
Sorrow has left his life;
It will never return.

Him I call a brahmin,
Free from *I, me,* and *mine,*
Who knows the rise and fall of life.
He will not fall asleep again.

Him I call a brahmin
Whose way no one can know.
He lives free from past and future;
He lives free from decay and death.

The Brahmin
143

Possessing nothing, desiring nothing
For his own pleasure, his own profit,
He has become a force for good,
Working for the freedom of all.

He has reached the end of the way;
He has crossed the river of life.
All that he had to do is done;
He has become one with all life.

Part Five

The City of Brahman

In the city of Brahman is a secret dwelling,
the lotus of the heart. Within this dwelling
is a space, and within that space is the
fulfillment of our desires. What is within
that space should be longed for and realized.

As great as the infinite space beyond is the
space within the lotus of the heart. Both
heaven and earth are contained in that inner
space, both fire and air, sun and moon,
lightning and stars. Whether we know it
in this world or know it not, everything is
contained in that inner space.

Never fear that old age will invade that
city; never fear that this inner treasure of all
reality will wither and decay. This knows
no age when the body ages; this knows no
dying when the body dies. This is the real
city of Brahman; this is the Self, free from
old age, from death and grief, hunger and
thirst. In the Self all desires are fulfilled.

The Self desires only what is real, thinks nothing but what is true. Here people do what they are told, becoming dependent on their country, or their piece of land, or the desires of another, so their desires are not fulfilled and their works come to nothing, both in this world and in the next. Those who depart from this world without knowing who they are or what they truly desire have no freedom here or hereafter.

But those who leave here knowing who they are and what they truly desire have freedom everywhere, both in this world and in the next.

Like strangers in an unfamiliar country walking over a hidden treasure, day by day we enter the world of Brahman while in deep sleep but never find it, carried away by what is false.

The Self is hidden in the lotus of the heart. Those who see themselves in all creatures go day by day into the world of Brahman hidden in the heart. Established in peace, they rise above body-consciousness to the supreme light of the Self. Immortal, free from fear, this Self is Brahman, called the True. Beyond the mortal and the immortal,

he binds both worlds together. Those who
know this live day after day in heaven in this
very life.

The Self is a bulwark against the confound-
ing of these worlds and a bridge between
them. Day and night cannot cross that
bridge, nor old age, nor death, nor grief,
nor evil or good deeds. All evils turn back
there, unable to cross; evil comes not into
this world of Brahman.

One who crosses by this bridge, therefore,
if blind, is blind no more; if hurt, ceases
to be hurt; if in sorrow, ceases sorrowing.
At this boundary night itself becomes
day: night comes not into this world
of Brahman.

Only those who are pure and self-controlled
can find this world of Brahman. That world
is theirs alone. In that world, in all the
worlds, they live in perfect freedom.

The Island

For those struggling in midstream,
in great fear of the flood, of growing old and of dying – for all those
I say, an island exists where there is
no place for impediments, no place
for clinging: the island of no going
beyond.

I call it nirvana, the complete
destruction of old age and dying.

In the Midst of Darkness

I do dimly perceive that whilst everything around
me is ever changing, ever dying, there is underlying
all that change a living power that is changeless,
that holds all together, that creates, dissolves, and
re-creates. That informing power or spirit is God.
And since nothing else that I see merely through
the senses can or will persist, He alone is.

And is this power benevolent or malevolent? I see
it as purely benevolent. For I can see that in the midst
of death life persists, in the midst of untruth truth
persists, in the midst of darkness light persists. Hence
I gather that God is Life, Truth, Light. He is Love.
He is the Supreme Good.

What Is Real Never Ceases

The Self dwells in the house of the body,
Which passes through childhood, youth, and old age.
So passes the Self at the time of death
Into another body. The wise know this truth
And are not deceived by it.

When the senses come in contact with sense-objects
They give rise to feelings of heat and cold,
Pleasure and pain, which come and go.
Accept them calmly, as do the wise.

The wise, who live free from pleasure and pain,
Are worthy of immortality.

What is real never ceases to be.
The unreal never is. The sages
Who realize the Self know the secret
Of what is and what is not.

Know that the Self, the ground of existence,
Can never be destroyed or diminished.
For the changeless cannot be changed.

Bodies die, not the Self that dwells therein.
Know the Self to be beyond change and death.
Therefore strive to realize this Self.

Those who look upon the Self as slayer
Or as slain have not realized the Self.
How can the Self be killed or kill
When there is only One?

Never was the Self born; never shall it
Cease to be. Without beginning or end,
Free from birth, free from death, and free from time,
How can the Self die when the body dies?

Who knows the Self to be birthless, deathless,
Not subject to the tyranny of time,
How can the Self slay or cause to be slain?

Even as we cast off worn-out garments
And put on new ones, so casts off the Self
A worn-out body and enters into
Another that is new.

Not pierced by arrows nor burnt by fire,
Affected by neither water nor wind,
The Self is not a physical creature.

Not wounded, not burnt, not wetted, not dried,
The Self is ever and everywhere,
Immovable and everlasting.

The Self cannot be known by the senses,
Nor thought by the mind, nor caught by time.
If you know this, you will not grieve.

Even if you mistake the Self to be
Subject to birth and death, you must not grieve.
For death is certain for those who are born,
As rebirth is certain for those who die.
Why grieve over what cannot be avoided?

We perceive creatures only after birth,
And after they die we perceive them not.
They are manifest only between birth
And death. In this there is no cause for grief.

Some there are who have realized the Self
In all its wonder. Others can speak of it
As wonderful. But there are many
Who don't understand even when they hear.

Deathless is the Self in every creature.
Know this truth, and leave all sorrow behind.

The Lord of Life

May we harness body and mind to see
The Lord of Life who dwells in everyone.
May we with one-pointed mind
Ever strive for blissful union with the Lord.
May our senses through meditation be
Trained to serve the Lord of Life.

Great is the glory of the Lord of Life,
Infinite, omnipresent, all-knowing.
He is known by the wise who meditate
And conserve their vital energy.

Hear, O children of immortal bliss,
You are born to be united with the Lord.
Follow the path of the illumined ones,
And be united with the Lord of Life.

Ignite kundalini in the depths of
Meditation. Bring your breathing and mind
Under control. Drink deep of divine love,
And you will attain the unitive state.

Dedicate yourself to the Lord of Life,
Who is the cause of the cosmos. He will
Remove the cause of all your suffering
And free you from the bondage of karma.

Be seated with spinal column erect
And deep inwards turn the senses and mind.
With the mantram reverberating in
Your mind, cross the dread sea of birth and death.

Train the senses to be obedient.
Regulate your activities to lead you
To the goal. Hold the reins of your mind
As you hold the reins of restive horses.

Choose a place for meditation that is
Clean, quiet, and cool, a cave with a smooth floor
Without stones and dust, protected against
Wind and rain and pleasing to the eye.

In deep meditation aspirants may
See forms like snow or smoke. They may feel
A strong wind blowing or a wave of heat.
They may see within them more and more light,
Fireflies, lightning, sun, or moon. These are signs
That they are well on their way to Brahman.

Health, a light body, freedom from cravings,
Clear skin, sonorous voice, a pleasant odor:
These are signs of progress in meditation.

As a dusty mirror shines bright when cleansed,
So shines the one who realizes the Self,
Attains life's goal, and passes beyond sorrow.

In the supreme climax of samadhi
He realizes the presence of the Lord
In his consciousness and is freed from all
Impurities — he the pure and deathless.

The Lord dwells in the womb of the cosmos,
The Creator who is in all creatures.
He is that which is born and to be born;
His face is everywhere.

Let us adore the Lord of Life, who is
Present in fire and water, plants and trees.
Let us adore the Lord of Life!
Let us adore the Lord of Life!

The Lord Is My Shepherd

The Lord is my shepherd;
    I shall not want.
He maketh me to lie down in green pastures:
    He leadeth me beside the still waters.
He restoreth my soul:
    He leadeth me in the paths of righteousness
    for his name's sake.
Yea, though I walk
    through the valley of the shadow of death,
I will fear no evil:
    for thou art with me;
Thy rod and thy staff they comfort me.
Thou preparest a table before me
    in the presence of mine enemies:
Thou anointest my head with oil;
    my cup runneth over.
Surely goodness and mercy shall follow me
    all the days of my life:
And I will dwell in the house of the Lord
    for ever.

The Ruler Within

THE KING OF DEATH:

There is a city with eleven gates
Of which the ruler is the unborn Self,
Whose light forever shines.
They go beyond sorrow who meditate on the Self
And are freed from the cycle of birth and death.
For this Self is supreme!

The Self is the sun shining in the sky,
The wind blowing in space; he is the fire
At the altar and in the home the guest;
He dwells in human beings, in gods, in truth,
And in the vast firmament; he is the fish
Born in water, the plant growing in the earth,
The river flowing down from the mountain.
For this Self is supreme!

The adorable one who is seated
In the heart rules the breath of life.
Unto him all the senses pay their homage.
When the dweller in the body breaks out
In freedom from the bonds of flesh, what remains?
For this Self is supreme!
We live not by the breath that flows in
And flows out, but by him who causes the breath
To flow in and flow out.

Now, O Nachiketa, I will tell you
Of this unseen, eternal Brahman, and
What befalls the Self after death.
Of those unaware of the Self, some are born
As embodied creatures while others remain
In a lower stage of evolution,
As determined by their own need for growth.

That which is awake even in our sleep,
Giving form in dreams to the objects of
Sense craving, that indeed is pure light,
Brahman the immortal, who contains all
The cosmos, and beyond whom none can go.
For this Self is supreme!

As the same fire assumes different shapes
When it consumes objects differing in shape,
So does the one Self take the shape
Of every creature in whom he is present.
As the same air assumes different shapes
When it enters objects differing in shape,
So does the one Self take the shape
Of every creature in whom he is present.

As the sun, who is the eye of the world,
Cannot be tainted by the defects in our eyes
Or by the objects it looks on,
So the one Self, dwelling in all, cannot
Be tainted by the evils of the world.
For this Self transcends all!

The ruler supreme, inner Self of all,
Multiplies his oneness into many.
Eternal joy is theirs who see the Self
In their own hearts. To none else does it come!

Changeless amidst the things that pass away,
Pure consciousness in all who are conscious,
The One answers the prayers of many.
Eternal peace is theirs who see the Self
In their own hearts. To none else does it come!

NACHIKETA:
How can I know that blissful Self, supreme,
Inexpressible, realized by the wise?
Is he the light, or does he reflect light?

THE KING OF DEATH:
There shines not the sun, neither moon nor star,
Nor flash of lightning, nor fire lit on earth.
The Self is the light reflected by all.
He shining, everything shines after him.

Let Me Walk In Beauty

O Great Spirit,
>   whose voice I hear in the winds
>   and whose breath gives life to all the world,
>   hear me.

I am small and weak.
I need your strength and wisdom.
Let me walk in beauty
>   and let my eyes ever behold the red and purple sunset.

Make my hands respect the things you have made
>   and my ears grow sharp to hear your voice.

Make me wise so that I may understand the things
>   you have taught my people.

Let me learn the lessons you have hidden
>   in every leaf and rock.

I seek strength not to be greater than my brother or sister
>   but to fight my greatest enemy, myself.

Make me always ready
>   to come to you with clean hands and straight eyes

So when life fades as the fading sunset
>   my spirit may come to you without shame.

Great Spirit of love,
>   come to me with the power of the North.

Make me courageous when the cold winds of life fall
>   upon me.

Give me strength and endurance for everything
that is harsh,
everything that hurts,
everything that makes me squint.
Make me move through life ready to take what comes
from the North.

Spirit who comes out of the East,
come to me with the power of the rising sun.
Let there be light in my word.
Let there be light on the path that I walk.
Let me remember always that you give the gift of a
new day.
Never let me be burdened with sorrow by not
starting over.

Great Spirit of creation,
send me the warm and soothing winds
from the South.
Comfort me and caress me when I am tired and cold.
Enfold me as your gentle breezes enfold your leaves
on the trees.
And as you give to all the earth your warm,
moving wind,
Give to me so that I may grow close to you in warmth.
Great life-giving Spirit,
I face the West,
the direction of the sundown.
Let me remember every day that the moment will come
when my sun will go down.
Never let me forget that I must fade into you.
Give me beautiful color.
Give me a great sky for setting,
and when it is time to meet you,
I come with glory.

And Giver of all life, I pray to you from the earth,
    help me to remember as I touch the earth
    that I am little and need your pity.
Help me to be thankful for the gift of the earth
    and never to walk hurtfully on the world.
Bless to love what comes from mother earth
    and teach me how to love your gifts.

Great Spirit of the heavens,
    lift me up to you
    that my heart may worship you
    and come to you in glory.
Hold in my memory that you are my Creator,
    greater than I,
    eager for my good life.
Let everything that is in the world
    lift my mind,
    and my heart,
    and my life to you
    so that we may come always to you
        in truth and in heart.

Four Things That Bring Much Inward Peace

– My child, now will I teach thee the way of peace and true liberty.

– O Lord, I beseech thee, do as thou sayest, for this is delightful for me to hear.

– Be desirous, my child, to work for the welfare of another rather than seek thine own will.

Choose always to have less rather than more.

Seek always the lowest place, and to be inferior to everyone.

Wish always, and pray, that the will of God may be wholly fulfilled in thee.

Behold, such a man entereth within the borders of peace and rest.

– O Lord, this short discourse of thine containeth within itself much perfection. It is little to be spoken, but full of meaning, and abundant in fruit. . . . Thou who canst do all things, and ever lovest the profiting of my soul, increase in me thy grace, that I may be able to fulfill thy words, and to work out mine own salvation.

The Tree of Eternity

The Tree of Eternity has its roots above
And its branches on earth below.
Its pure root is Brahman the immortal,
From whom all the worlds draw their life, and whom
None can transcend. For this Self is supreme!

The cosmos comes forth from Brahman and moves
In him. With his power it reverberates,
Like thunder crashing in the sky. Those who realize him
Pass beyond the sway of death.

In fear of him fire burns; in fear of him
The sun shines, the clouds rain, and the winds blow.
In fear of him death stalks about to kill.

If one fails to realize Brahman in this life
Before the physical sheath is shed,
He must again put on a body
In the world of embodied creatures.

Brahman can be seen, as in a mirror,
In a pure heart; in the world of the ancestors
As in a dream; in the gandharva world
As the reflections in trembling waters;
And clear as light in the realm of the Creator.

Knowing the senses to be separate
From the Self, and the sense experience
To be fleeting, the wise grieve no more.

Above the senses is the mind,
Above the mind is the intellect, above that
Is the ego, and above the ego
Is the unmanifested Cause.
And beyond is Brahman, omnipresent,
Attributeless. Realizing him one is released
From the cycle of birth and death.

He is formless, and can never be seen
With these two eyes. But he reveals himself
In the heart made pure through meditation
And sense-restraint. Realizing him one is released
From the cycle of birth and death.

When the five senses are stilled, when the mind
Is stilled, when the intellect is stilled,
That is called the highest state by the wise.
They say yoga is this complete stillness
In which one enters the unitive state,
Never to become separate again.
If one is not established in this state,
The sense of unity will come and go.

The unitive state cannot be attained
Through words or thoughts or through the eye.
How can it be attained except through one who is
Established in this state himself?

There are two selves, the separate ego
And the indivisible Atman.
When one rises above *I, me,* and *mine,*
The Atman is revealed as one's real Self.

When all desires that surge in the heart
Are renounced, the mortal becomes immortal.
When all the knots that strangle the heart
Are loosened, the mortal becomes immortal.
This sums up the teaching of the scriptures.

From the heart there radiate a hundred
And one vital tracks. One of them rises
To the crown of the head. This way leads
To immortality, the others to death.

The Lord of Love, not larger than the thumb,
Is ever enshrined in the hearts of all.
Draw him clear out of the physical sheath,
As one draws the stalk from the munja grass.
Know thyself to be pure and immortal!
Know thyself to be pure and immortal!

O M *Shanti Shanti Shanti*

Epistle on Love

If I speak in the tongues of men and and of angels, but
have not love, I am a noisy gong or a clanging cymbal.
And if I have prophetic powers, and understand all
mysteries and all knowledge, and if I have all faith, so as
to remove mountains, but have not love, I am nothing.
If I give away all I have, and if I deliver my body to be
burned, but have not love, I gain nothing.

Love is patient and kind; love is not jealous or boastful;
it is not arrogant or rude. Love does not insist on its own
way; it is not irritable or resentful; it does not rejoice at
wrong, but rejoices in the right. Love bears all things,
believes all things, hopes all things, endures all things.

Love never ends; as for prophecies, they will pass away;
as for tongues, they will cease; as for knowledge, it will
pass away. For our knowledge is imperfect and our
prophecy is imperfect; but when the perfect comes, the
imperfect will pass away.

When I was a child, I spoke like a child, I thought like
a child, I reasoned like a child; when I became a man, I
gave up childish ways. For now we see in a mirror dimly,
but then face to face. Now I know in part; then I shall understand fully, even as I have been fully understood.

So faith, hope, love abide, these three; but the greatest of
these is love.

The Way of Peace

When the good God calls us in this world, he finds us full of vices and sins, and his first work is to give us the instinct to practice virtue; then he incites us to desire perfection, and afterwards, by infused grace, he conducts us to the true self-naughting, and finally to the true transformation. This is the extraordinary road along which God conducts the soul. But when the soul is thus naughted and transformed, it no longer works, or speaks, or wills, or feels, or understands, nor has it in itself any knowledge, either of that which is internal or external, which could possibly affect it; and, in all these things God is its director and guide without the help of any creature.

In this state, the soul is in such peace and tranquillity that it seems to her that both soul and body are immersed in a sea of the profoundest peace, from which she would not issue for anything that could happen in this life. She remains immovable, imperturbable, and neither her humanity nor her spirit feels anything except the sweetest peace, of which she is so full, that if her flesh, her bones, her nerves were pressed, nothing would issue from them but peace. And all day long she sings softly to herself for joy, saying: *"Shall I show thee what God is? No one finds peace apart from him."*

Entering into Joy

Imagine if all the tumult of the body were to quiet down,
along with all our busy thoughts about earth, sea, and air;

if the very world should stop, and the mind cease thinking about itself, go beyond itself, and be quite still;

if all the fantasies that appear in dreams and imagination
should cease, and there be no speech, no sign:

Imagine if all things that are perishable grew still –
for if we listen they are saying, *We did not make ourselves;
he made us who abides forever* – imagine, then, that they
should say this and fall silent, listening to the very voice
of him who made them and not to that of his creation;

so that we should hear not his word through the tongues
of men, nor the voice of angels, nor the clouds' thunder,
nor any symbol, but the very Self which in these things
we love, and go beyond ourselves to attain a flash of that
eternal wisdom which abides above all things:

And imagine if that moment were to go on and on,
leaving behind all other sights and sounds but this one
vision which ravishes and absorbs and fixes the beholder
in joy; so that the rest of eternal life were like that
moment of illumination which leaves us breathless:

Would this not be what is bidden in scripture, *Enter thou
into the joy of thy Lord?*

You Are That

This is the teaching of Uddalaka to Shvetaketu, his son:

As by knowing one lump of clay, dear one,
We come to know all things made out of clay –
That they differ only in name and form,
While the stuff of which all are made is clay;

As by knowing one gold nugget, dear one,
We come to know all things made out of gold –
That they differ only in name and form,
While the stuff of which all are made is gold;

As by knowing one tool of iron, dear one,
We come to know all things made out of iron –
That they differ only in name and form,
While the stuff of which all are made is iron –

So through spiritual wisdom, dear one,
We come to know that all of life is one.

In the beginning was only Being,
One without a second.
Out of himself he brought forth the cosmos
And entered into everything in it.
There is nothing that does not come from him.
Of everything he is the inmost Self.
He is the truth; he is the Self supreme.
You are that, Shvetaketu; you are that.

When a person is absorbed in dreamless sleep
He is one with the Self, though he knows it not.
We say he sleeps, but he sleeps in the Self.
As a tethered bird grows tired of flying
About in vain to find a place of rest
And settles down at last on its own perch,
So the mind, tired of wandering about
Hither and thither, settles down at last
In the Self, dear one, to whom it is bound.
All creatures, dear one, have their source in him.
He is their home; he is their strength.
There is nothing that does not come from him.
Of everything he is the inmost Self.
He is the truth; he is the Self supreme.
You are that, Shvetaketu; you are that.

As bees suck nectar from many a flower
And make their honey one, so that no drop
Can say, "I am from this flower or that,"
All creatures, though one, know not they are that One.
There is nothing that does not come from him.
Of everything he is the inmost Self.
He is the truth; he is the Self supreme.
You are that, Shvetaketu; you are that.

As the rivers flowing east and west
Merge in the sea and become one with it,
Forgetting they were ever separate streams,
So do all creatures lose their separateness
When they merge at last into pure Being.
There is nothing that does not come from him.
Of everything he is the inmost Self.
He is the truth; he is the Self supreme.
You are that, Shvetaketu; you are that!

Let Nothing Upset You

Let nothing upset you;
Let nothing frighten you.
Everything is changing;
God alone is changeless.
Patience attains the goal.
Who has God lacks nothing;
God alone fills every need.

Prayer for Peace

Adorable presence,
Thou who art within and without,
    above and below and all around,
Thou who art interpenetrating
    every cell of my being,
Thou who art the eye of my eyes,
    the ear of my ears,
    the heart of my heart,
    the mind of my mind,
    the breath of my breath,
    the life of my life,
    the soul of my soul,
Bless us, dear God, to be aware of thy presence
    now and here.

May we all be aware of thy presence
    in the East and the West,
    in the North and the South.
May peace and good will abide among individuals,
    communities, and nations.
This is my earnest prayer.

May peace be unto all!

May the thread of my song
be not cut before my life
merges in the sea of love.

The Message of the Scriptures

Every morning my spiritual teacher, my grandmother, used to go to our ancestral temple to worship the Lord as Shiva. On her return she would place behind my ear a flower she had offered to the Lord in worship and bless me with these simple words: "May you be like Markandeya!"

Markandeya is an illumined teenager in the Hindu scriptures, whose parents prayed for a son who would be completely devoted to Lord Shiva. Their prayer was finally granted – but with the sad condition that their son would die on his sixteenth birthday.

The first word Markandeya lisped as a baby was "Shiva, Shiva." His love for the Lord grew from day to day until it filled his consciousness. When he attained his sixteenth birthday, he learned from his heartbroken parents that Yama, the King of Death, would be claiming him as his victim that day. On hearing this, Markandeya sat down in deep meditation at the feet of Lord Shiva, who is known in Sanskrit as *Mrityunjaya,* the Conqueror of Death.

At the appointed hour, Yama appeared for his victim. But as he was about to carry him away, Lord Shiva arose in the depths of Markandeya's meditation to protect his young devotee. The Lord placed one hand on Markandeya's head in infinite love, and with the other he pointed his trident at the King of Death, who trembled like a leaf in the wind at the sight of Mrityunjaya.

"Don't you know," asked the Conqueror of Death, "that anyone who takes refuge at my feet has gone beyond your power? Markandeya has now become immortal through my grace."

It took years for me to understand that Markandeya's story is not poetry, fantasy, or philosophy. It is possible for every human being to go beyond the reach of death, not in some afterlife but here and now. And not only is it possible, it is our birthright.

This realization lies at the heart of mysticism everywhere. The instruction in the Bhagavad Gita and the Upanishads is clear, complete, and practical. You are neither body nor mind, both of which are subject to change. The body is your external instrument; the mind is your internal instrument. But you are the operator, the *Atman* or Self. This Self is immutable, immortal, indivisible, infinite, the same in every creature. To realize the Self is to attain the supreme goal of life.

This is the purpose of meditation. Self-realization is beyond the senses and the intellect. It comes through a higher mode of knowing, developed through the sincere, systematic, sustained practice of meditation over many years. When the senses are stilled, when the mind is stilled, you are enabled through the infinite love of the Lord to become united with him in the supreme state of *samadhi*. To attain samadhi is to pass beyond death, to realize that you are immortal.

This deathless state of Self-realization can be attained by you while you are living right here on the face of this earth. As the medieval mystic Kabir puts it:

> O friend, know him and be one with him whilst you live.
> If you know him not in life, how can you in death?
> Don't dream that your soul will be united with him
> Because the body-house is demolished by death.
> If he is realized now, he is realized then too;
> If not, you go but to live in the Land of Death.

Lord Shiva is represented traditionally as the Divine Beggar, who comes with his begging bowl to your door for alms. When you offer this beggar food, clothes, money, he refuses to accept them.

"What do you want from me then?" you ask.

"Your ego," comes the answer: "your selfishness, your

separateness. Throw that in my bowl and become united with Mrityunjaya, Conqueror of Death."

The scriptures describe Lord Shiva as seated in *sahasrara*, the thousand-petalled lotus, which may well be a spiritual symbol for the millions of cells that make up the human brain. In deep meditation there are many remarkable experiences that make you aware of this thousand-petalled lotus blooming in all its glory. In the stupendous climax of *samadhi*, you are enabled to wake up from the dream of being just a separate petal into the realization that you are the whole lotus, with the Lord of Love enshrined within it.

This is the message of every major scripture. It is the testimony of mystics everywhere, East or West. So I would like to offer this little anthology with the same blessing I received from my grandmother, which still reverberates through my life: *Meditate. Realize the Self. Transcend death here and now. Become like Markandeya!*

EKNATH EASWARAN
An Eight-Point Program

When I came to this country as an exchange professor in 1959, I was invited to speak to many groups of people on the source of India's ancient civilization. At the end of every talk a few thoughtful men and women would come up and ask me, "How can we bring these changeless values into our own daily life?"

"You don't have to change your religion," I assured them, "to do what I have done. The method of meditation I learned is universal. It can be practiced within the mainstream of any religious tradition, and outside all of them as well."

I began by teaching simply what I myself had been practicing for over a decade, illustrating from the scriptures and mystics of the world's great religions. Very quickly this became systematized into eight points, the first and most important of which is meditation. The next few pages are a short introduction to this eight-point program for spiritual growth, which is discussed fully in my book *Meditation*.

1. Meditation

The heart of this program is meditation: half an hour every morning, as early as is convenient. Do not increase this period; if you want to meditate more, have half an hour in the evening also, preferably at the very end of the day.

Set aside a room in your home to be used only for meditation and spiritual reading. After a while that room will become associated with meditation in your mind, so that simply entering it will have a calming effect. If you cannot spare a room, have a particular corner. Whichever you choose, keep your meditation place clean, well ventilated, and reasonably austere.

Sit in a straight-backed chair or on the floor and gently close your eyes. If you sit on the floor, you may need to support your back lightly against a wall. You should be comfortable enough to forget your body, but not so comfortable that you become drowsy.

Whatever position you choose, be sure to keep your head, neck, and spinal column erect in a straight line. As concentration deepens, the nervous system relaxes and you may begin to fall asleep. It is important to resist this tendency right from the beginning, by drawing yourself up and away from your back support until the wave of sleep has passed.

Once you have closed your eyes, begin to go *slowly,* in your mind, through one of the passages from the scriptures or the great mystics which I recommend for use in meditation. I usually suggest learning first the Prayer of Saint Francis of Assisi.

In memorizing the prayer, it may be helpful to remind yourself that you are not addressing some extraterrestrial being outside you. The kingdom of heaven is within us, and the Lord is enshrined in the depths of our own consciousness. In this prayer we are calling deep into ourselves, appealing to the spark of the divine that is our real nature.

While you are meditating, do not follow any association of ideas or try to think about the passage. If you are giving your attention to each word, the meaning cannot help sinking in. When distractions come, do not resist them, but give more attention to the words of the passage. If your mind strays from the passage entirely, bring it back gently to the beginning and start again.

When you reach the end of the passage, you may use it again as necessary to complete your period of meditation until you have memorized others. It is helpful to have a wide variety of passages for meditation, drawn from the world's major traditions. Each passage should be positive and practical, drawn from a major scripture or from a mystic of the highest stature.

The secret of meditation is simple: we become what we meditate on. When you use the Prayer of Saint Francis every day in meditation, you are driving the words deep into your consciousness. Eventually they become an integral part of your personality, which means they will find constant expression in what you do, what you say, and what you think.

2. Repetition of the Mantram

A mantram, or Holy Name, is a powerful spiritual formula which has the capacity to transform consciousness when it is repeated silently in the mind. There is nothing magical about this. It is simply a matter of practice, as you can verify for yourself.

Every religious tradition has a mantram, often more than one. For Christians, the name of Jesus itself is a powerful mantram. Catholics also use *Hail Mary* or *Ave Maria.* Jews may use *Barukh attah Adonai,* "Blessed art thou, O Lord," or the Hasidic formula *Ribono shel olam,* "Lord of the universe." Muslims repeat the name of Allah or *Allahu akbar,* "God is great." Probably the oldest Buddhist mantram is *Om mani padme hum,* referring to the "jewel in the lotus of the heart." In Hinduism, among many choices, I recommend *Rama, Rama, Rama,* which was Mahatma Gandhi's mantram.

Select a mantram that appeals to you deeply. In many traditions it is customary to take the mantram used by your spiritual teacher. Then, once you have chosen, do not change your mantram. Otherwise you will be like a person digging shallow holes in many places; you will never go deep enough to find water.

Repeat your mantram silently whenever you get the chance: while walking, while waiting, while you are doing mechanical chores like washing dishes, and especially when you are falling asleep. You will find for yourself that this is not mindless repetition. The mantram will help to keep you relaxed and alert during the day, and when you can fall asleep in it, it will go on working for you throughout the night as well.

Whenever you are angry or afraid, nervous or worried or resentful, repeat the mantram until the agitation subsides. The mantram works to steady the mind, and all these emotions are power running against you which the mantram can harness and put to work.

3. Slowing Down

Hurry makes for tension, insecurity, inefficiency, and superficial living. I believe that it also makes for illness: among other things, "hurry sickness" is a major component of the Type A behavior pattern which research has linked to heart disease. To guard against hurrying through the day, start the day early and simplify your life so that you do not try to fill your time with more than you can do. When you find yourself beginning to speed up, repeat your mantram to help you slow down.

It is important here not to confuse slowness with sloth, which breeds carelessness, procrastination, and general inefficiency. In slowing down we should attend meticulously to details, giving our very best even to the smallest undertaking.

4. One-pointed Attention

Doing more than one thing at a time divides attention and fragments consciousness. When we read and eat at the same time, for example, part of our mind is on what we are reading and part on what we are eating; we are not getting the most from either activity. Similarly, when talking with someone, give that person your full attention. These are little things, but all together they help to unify consciousness and deepen concentration.

Everything we do should be worthy of our full attention. When the mind is one-pointed it will be secure, free from tension, and capable of the concentration that is the mark of genius in any field.

5. Training the Senses

In the food we eat, the books and magazines we read, the movies we see, all of us are subject to the conditioning of rigid likes and dislikes. To free ourselves from this conditioning, we need to learn to change our likes and dislikes freely when it is in the best interests of those around us or ourselves. We should choose what we eat by what our body needs, for example, rather than by what the taste buds demand. Similarly, the mind eats too, through the senses. In this age of mass media, we need to be particularly discriminating in what we read and what we go to see for entertainment, for we become in part what our senses take in.

6. Putting Others First

Dwelling on ourselves builds a wall between ourselves and others. Those who keep thinking about *their* needs, *their* wants, *their* plans, *their* ideas cannot help becoming lonely and insecure. The simple but effective technique I recommend is to learn to put other people first — beginning within the circle of your family and friends, where there is already a basis of love on which to build. When husband and wife try to put each other first, for example, they are not only moving closer to each other. They are also removing the barriers of their ego-prison, which deepens their relationships with everyone else as well.

7. Reading in World Mysticism

We are so surrounded today by a low concept of what the human being is that it is essential to give ourselves a higher image. For this reason I recommend devoting half an hour or so each day to reading the scriptures and the writings of the great mystics of all religions. Just before bedtime, after evening meditation, is a particularly good time, because the thoughts you fall asleep in will be with you throughout the night.

There is a helpful distinction between works of inspiration and works of spiritual instruction. Inspiration may be drawn from every tradition or religion. Instructions in meditation and other spiritual disciplines, however, can differ from and even seem to contradict each other. For this reason, it is wise to confine instructional reading to the works of one teacher or path. Choose your teacher carefully. A good teacher lives what he or she teaches, and it is the student's responsibility to exercise sound judgment. Then, once you have chosen, give your teacher your full loyalty.

8. Spiritual Association

The Sanskrit word for this is *satsang,* "association with those who are spiritually oriented." When we are trying to change our life, we need the support of others with the same goal. If you have friends who are meditating along the lines suggested here, it is a great help to meditate together regularly. Share your times of entertainment too; relaxation is an important part of spiritual living.

★

This eightfold program, if it is followed sincerely and systematically, begins to transform personality almost immediately, leading to profoundly beneficial changes which spread to those around us.

Notes on the Passages

29   PRAYER OF SAINT FRANCIS   Francis Bernadone, perhaps the most universally loved of Christian saints, was born in Assisi, Italy, in 1181 or 1182. At the age of twenty-two, after a sudden illness that brought him almost to the point of death, he left his home and inheritance to follow an injunction that he felt he received from Christ himself: "Francis, go and rebuild my Church." Three great Franciscan orders quickly grew around the monks, nuns, and lay disciples who responded to his joyful example of universal love and selfless service.

30   INVOCATIONS TO THE UPANISHADS   The Upanishads are probably the oldest mystical documents in the world. In written form they date from the second century before Christ; how long they were preserved before that in India's long oral tradition can only be conjectured. The invocations in this collection are associated with various Upanishads, often with more than one. Selections 1 and 2 have been translated by Eknath Easwaran; the others are from *The Upanishads: Breath of the Eternal,* translated by Swami Prabhavananda and Frederick Manchester (Hollywood: Vedanta Press, 1968).

34   THE SHEMA   These segments of the Torah have been recited together since Biblical times as the central affirmation of the Jewish faith. Tradition prescribes that the Shema be spoken "with entire collection and concentration of heart and mind." This translation is by Ellen Lehmann Beeler.

35   HYMN TO THE DIVINE MOTHER   In the Hindu tradition the Lord is often regarded as possessing two aspects, one masculine, the other feminine. The latter, the creative power of the Godhead, is worshipped under

several names as the Divine Mother of the universe. The hymn in this book is taken from the Chandi, a sacred book which sings the praise of the Divine Mother. The translation is by Swami Prabhavananda and Christopher Isherwood, from *Prayers and Meditations Compiled from the Scriptures of India* (Hollywood: Vedanta Press, 1967).

36 THE ILLUMINED MAN   These are the closing verses of the second chapter of the Bhagavad Gita ("Song of the Lord"), India's best-known scripture, a masterpiece of world poetry on which countless mystics have drawn for daily practical guidance. The Gita is a dialogue between Sri Krishna, an incarnation of the Lord, and his friend and disciple Arjuna, a warrior prince who represents anyone trying to live a spiritual life in the midst of worldly activity and conflict. This translation is by Eknath Easwaran, from his *Bhagavad Gita for Daily Living* (Petaluma, California: Nilgiri Press, 1975–85).

38 FINDING UNITY   Chapter 56 of the Tao Te Ching, a collection of verses about Tao – "the Way," the indivisible unity of life – traditionally ascribed to the great Chinese mystic Lao Tzu, who lived perhaps in the sixth century B.C. This translation is by Stephen Ruppenthal.

39 I GAVE ALL MY HEART   Teresa de Cepeda y Ahumada, born in Avila, Spain, in 1515, is one of the best-loved saints in the Catholic tradition and a spiritual figure of universal appeal. A vivacious, talented girl, she entered a Carmelite convent at eighteen and passed more than twenty years there in doubt and division before she was able to dedicate herself completely to God. After that, her life is one of intense practical activity – establishing convents, teaching, writing, traveling – centered in the deepest spirituality and inner peace. Her three books are classics of world mysticism. These little poems were written without thought of publication.

40 PRAYERS FROM THE RIG VEDA   The Rig Veda contains the most ancient portions of the Hindu scriptures. Hymns, from which these two selections have been chosen, make up the first part of each Veda; in the latter parts are found the Upanishads (see notes for page 30). "God Makes the Rivers to Flow" has been translated by Eknath

Easwaran; "May We Be United in Heart," translated by Swami Prabhavananda and Christopher Isherwood, is from *Prayers and Meditations Compiled from the Scriptures of India* (Hollywood: Vedanta Press, 1967).

42   THE MIRACLE OF ILLUMINATION   From the *Bodhicharyavatara* of Shantideva, a Buddhist saint of the seventh century. *Bodhi,* "illumination," comes from the Sanskrit root *buddh,* "to wake up"; *dharma* is the law of unity that underlies all life. This is a free rendering for meditation by Eknath Easwaran.

43   TWIN VERSES   This is the opening chapter of the Dhammapada, an ancient collection of the Buddha's teachings in verse form. *Buddha* – literally "he who is awake" – is the title given to the young prince Siddhartha Gautama (ca. 563–483 B.C.) after he attained *nirvana* or self-realization. The translation is by Eknath Easwaran, adapted for meditation from *The Dhammapada* (Petaluma, California: Nilgiri Press, 1985).

46   THE WONDERFUL EFFECTS OF DIVINE LOVE Selected from Book 3, Chapter 5, of *The Imitation of Christ,* a book that has probably been read by and inspired more Christians than any other spiritual work except the Bible. Its traditional author, Thomas a Kempis (ca. 1380–1471), spent most of his life in Holland among the Brethren of the Common Life, a community devoted to a life of simplicity, selfless service, and the "imitation of Christ" in tumultuous times that fostered other notable European mystics, including Saint Catherine of Siena, Henry Suso, and Nicholas of Cusa. This translation, based on that of Anthony Hoskins (ca. 1613), is from *Of the Imitation of Christ: Four Books by Thomas a Kempis,* The World's Classics, vol. 49 (London: Oxford University Press, 1903).

50   THE REAL LOVERS OF GOD   Mahatma Gandhi's favorite hymn from his own Hindu tradition, representing the highest ideal of the community to which he was born. This is a free rendering from the Gujarati of Narsinha Mehta (1414–1481) by Eknath Easwaran.

51   ONLY GOD I SAW   From a Persian ode by the eleventh century Sufi mystic Baba Kuhi of Shiraz. The

translation is from Reynold A. Nicholson, *The Mystics of Islam* (London: Arkana, 1989), copyright 1914 by Reynold A. Nicholson.

52 PERENNIAL JOY Part 1, canto 2, of the Katha Upanishad (see also notes for page 30). The Katha begins with the story of Nachiketa, a daring teenager who goes to the King of Death, Yama, to get the secret of life. The rest of the Upanishad gives Yama's teaching. This translation is by Eknath Easwaran, adapted for meditation from the version in his *Dialogue with Death: The Spiritual Psychology of the Katha Upanishad* (Petaluma: Nilgiri Press, 1981).

59 ADON OLAM *Adon Olam* ("Lord of the universe") is, after the Psalms, perhaps the most popular hymn in the Jewish liturgy. Authorship is ascribed to the poet and mystic Solomon ibn Gabirol, who lived in Spain in the eleventh century. This translation is by Ellen Lehmann Beeler.

60 DISCOURSE ON GOOD WILL From the Metta Sutta, part of the Sutta Nipata, a collection of dialogues with the Buddha said to be among the oldest parts of the Pali Buddhist canon. This translation is by Stephen Ruppenthal.

62 THE CENTRAL TRUTH Swami Ramdas was born Vittal Rao in Kerala, South India, in 1884 and took to the spiritual life when in his thirties. His long search for self-realization is vividly described in three of his books: *In Quest of God, In the Vision of God* (from which this passage was taken), and *World is God* (Bombay: Bharatiya Vidya Bhavan, 1969, 1963, and 1967).

63 THE WHOLE WORLD IS YOUR OWN These words are revered as the last message of Sri Sarada Devi (1853–1920), "Holy Mother," wife of Sri Ramakrishna (see notes for page 93) and helpmate in his work.

64 THE PRACTICE OF THE PRESENCE OF GOD Selections from a letter by "Brother Lawrence" (Nicholas Herman), who lived almost sixty years as an obscure lay brother among the Carmelites in seventeenth-century Paris. The little collection of letters and conversations known as *The Practice of the Presence of God,* pieced to-

gether after his death in 1691, less than a week after this
letter was written, is an underground classic of Christian
devotion.

66   HER HEART IS FULL OF JOY   See notes for page 39
on Saint Teresa of Avila. This is a free rendering by
Eknath Easwaran.

67   THE RAZOR'S EDGE   The Katha Upanishad, part 1,
canto 3 (see notes for page 52).

70   MOTHER OF ALL THINGS   Chapter 52 of the Tao Te
Ching (see notes for page 38).

71   INVOCATIONS   Abdullah al-Ansari, often referred to
as Ansari of Herat, was a Persian poet and mystic in the
Sufi tradition of Islam, who died in 1088. The verses col-
lected here have been translated by Sardar Sir Jogendra
Singh in *The Persian Mystics: Invocations of al-Ansari al-
Harawi* (London: J. Murray, 1939).

78   SIMPLE UNION   Kabir, a fifteenth-century Indian
mystic, is one of the world's great poets. He is often
claimed to be Hindu by the Hindus and Muslim by the
Muslims because of the way his songs infuse the mysticism of the Upanishads with the Sufis' ecstatic love, but
it would be truer to say he was too universal to be con-
fined to one tradition. This is a free rendering by Eknath
Easwaran.

79   THE WAY OF LOVE   Chapter 12 of the Bhagavad
Gita, translated by Eknath Easwaran (see entry for page
36 above).

82   BELOVED OF THE SOUL   Composed by Eleazar Ben
Moses Azikri, a sixteenth-century cabalist who lived in
Safed in upper Galilee. He and a few friends formed a pact
to dedicate themselves entirely to study of the scriptures
and worship of God, and this prayer was written for their
use. Published the year after he died, "Yedid Nefesh"
was so popular among Jewish communities all over the
Mediterranean that it became an accepted part of the Sab-
bath liturgy. This translation is by Rabbi Harvey Spivak.

83   THE INNER RULER   This is the whole of the Isha
Upanishad (see also the notes for page 30 above), which
Mahatma Gandhi said contains the summit of human

wisdom. Translated by Eknath Easwaran in *The Upanishads* (Petaluma, California: Nilgiri Press, 1987).

86 THE EARTH IS THE LORD'S
Psalm 24, King James Version.

87 SERVE THE LORD WITH GLADNESS
Psalm 100, King James Version.

88 THE SERMON ON THE MOUNT   From the Gospel According to Saint Matthew, 5:3–16, 43–48; 6:9–13 (King James Version).

93 SONGS OF SRI RAMAKRISHNA   Sri Ramakrishna, one of the great figures in world mysticism, was born in Bengal, North India, in 1836. He taught, and lived out in his own life, that God can be realized within any of the world's major religions if one seeks with completely unified desire. He worshipped God as the Divine Mother (see note for page 35 above). These songs, by different composers, are among the many that Sri Ramakrishna used to enjoy. They are selected from *The Gospel of Sri Ramakrishna,* by "M.", a disciple (New York: Ramakrishna-Vivekananda Center, 1942).

96 BELIEVING IN MIND   Seng Ts'an (third century B.C.) is said to have been the Third Patriarch of Ch'an Buddhism, which passed into Japan as Zen. This translation is by Stephen Ruppenthal.

98 THE HIDDEN SELF   This is the whole of the Amritabindu Upanishad (the name means "drop of the nectar of immortality"). *Brahman* refers to the ultimate reality, the supreme Godhead, beyond all distinctions or forms. Translated by Eknath Easwaran in *The Upanishads* (Petaluma, California: Nilgiri Press, 1987).

100 THE LAMP OF WISDOM   From the Yoga Vasishta (3:23–30), a dialogue between young prince Rama, a divine incarnation, and his spiritual teacher, the sage Vasishta. Vasishta discovers that the boy's apparent listlessness masks a preoccupation with the meaning of life and of death, and sets before him the lofty challenge of self-realization. This is a free rendering by Eknath Easwaran.

101 SHINE THROUGH US   There are several versions of this prayer in circulation, varying slightly to accommodate prayer by individuals or by groups, by Catholics or by non-Catholics. This is appropriate, for John Henry Newman lived fully half of his life as a Protestant, becoming well known as a speaker for the evangelical Oxford movement, and after his conversion in 1845 went on to become equally well known as Cardinal Newman, defender of the Catholic faith. This version is from Daphne Rae's book on Mother Teresa of Calcutta and the Missionaries of Charity, *Love Until It Hurts,* where it appears along with the prayer of Saint Francis as one of the daily prayers of this community dedicated to serving "the poorest of the poor."

'102 THE SHINING SELF   *Tejabindu* means "drop of splendor." The three stages of meditation referred to are *dharana, dhyana,* and finally *samadhi,* in which one realizes one's identity with the supreme reality. The *guna*s are the three qualities of the phenomenal world: *sattva,* law or virtue, *rajas,* passion or energy, and *tamas,* ignorance or inertia. Translated by Eknath Easwaran in *The Upanishads* (Petaluma, California: Nilgiri Press, 1987).

104 WHATEVER YOU DO   The concluding verses of Chapter 9 of the Bhagavad Gita, translated by Eknath Easwaran for use in meditation (see entry for page 36 above).

106 TEACH ME   Saint Anselm (1033–1109) was from northern Italy but came to Normandy and then to England as Archbishop of Canterbury. In the midst of heavy administrative duties he found time to write philosophical and theological treatises in defense of his faith. This passage appeals directly to the heart and needs no argument. The translation is from David A. Fleming, S.M., ed., *The Fire and the Cloud* (New York: Paulist Press, 1978).

107 THE ONE THING NEEDED   Tukaram, like Kabir (see notes for page 78), was a common man, a peasant farmer with no claim to learning, who represents the Bhakti school of Indian mysticism, the way of devotion. From

John S. Hoyland, *An Indian Peasant Mystic: Translations from Tukaram* (London, Allenson & Co., 1932).

108 THE BLESSING OF A WELL-TRAINED MIND The Dhammapada, chapter 4 (see notes for page 43). Mara (the name may come from the Sanskrit *mri,* "to die") is a personification of Death or Temptation, the sum of all the selfish attachments that bind one to a separate, self-centered existence. Translated by Eknath Easwaran in *The Dhammapada* (Petaluma, California: Nilgiri Press, 1986).

110 DUTIES OF THE HEART Written by Bahya ibn Paquda in Muslim Spain in the eleventh century, this passage is enduring proof of the beauty and power that can result when great cultures meet in the heart of a man or woman of God. Though written by a Jewish moral philosopher, "Duties of the Heart" was modeled on similar works of Muslim mystics and was meant to counterbalance the emphasis on ritual and ethical observances in the Jewish community. The original was written in Arabic and translated into Hebrew by Judah ibn Tibbon in 1161. This translation is by Rabbi Harvey Spivak.

112 THE UNSTRUCK BELLS AND DRUMS See notes for page 78, on Kabir.

113 JUST BECAUSE YOU ARE MY GOD Attributed to Saint Ignatius Loyola (1491–1556), founder of the Society of Jesus. Though he began life as a soldier, a long and very painful convalescence from a wound led to a spiritual transformation in which he turned his martial spirit and capacity for suffering to the service of the Lord. (Translator unknown.)

114 YOU ARE CHRIST'S HANDS Said to be from a letter by Saint Teresa of Avila to her nuns (see notes for page 39).

115 THE PATH Mohandas K. Gandhi – universally known as Mahatma Gandhi; the title means "great soul" – was born in British India in 1869 and died in January 1949, after having led his country to freedom through a nonviolent struggle based on love and selfless service. This passage is from a collection of his writings entitled *My Religion* (Ahmedabad, India: Navajivan, 1955).

116 BE AWARE OF ME ALWAYS   For practical purposes, these are the concluding verses of the Bhagavad Gita (18:49–73). The translation is by Eknath Easwaran, from *The Bhagavad Gita for Daily Living* (Petaluma, California: Nilgiri Press, 1975–85).

121 RADIANT IS THE WORLD SOUL   Rabbi Kook (1865–1935) is considered the foremost of modern Jewish mystics – a man of God who dealt with the practical problems of his people in a turbulent time while striving constantly to infuse their struggle with spiritual purpose. The translation is by Ben Zion Bokser, *Abraham Isaac Kook* (New York: Paulist Press, 1978).

122 LORD THAT GIVETH STRENGTH   From *The Imitation of Christ,* Book 3, Chapter 30 (see notes for page 46 above).

126 THE FRUIT OF THE TREE
127 WEAVING YOUR NAME
128 FORGIVENESS   See notes on Kabir for page 78.

129 THE RIVER OF GOD   From canto 1 of the Shvetashvatara Upanishad, one of the most beautiful of the Upanishads (see entry for page 30 above). It is dedicated to Shiva, the "Lord of Life," who represents God as the bestower of immortality. Translated by Eknath Easwaran in *The Upanishads* (Petaluma, California: Nilgiri Press, 1987).

132 THE BEST   The Tao Te Ching, chapter 8 (see notes for page 38). Translation by Stephen Ruppenthal.

133 THE PATH TO YOUR DWELLING
134 COME, BELOVED
135 LIFE OF MY LIFE   Meera was a Rajput princess in the sixteenth century. After her husband's death his family so persecuted her for her devotional practices that she left the palace and wandered on pilgrimage. Wherever she went she joined other devotees in singing and dancing in praise of the Lord. Her songs have been passed down by wandering minstrels who altered them to suit their native dialects. It is a testimony to their beauty and to the current of devotion in Indian life that they are still widely known and sung today. These are free renderings by Eknath Easwaran.

136 CHRIST BE WITH ME From a hymn traditionally ascribed to Saint Patrick.

138 THE SELF The Kena Upanishad (see also entry for page 30 above). *Kena* in Sanskrit means "by whom," the first word of the question with which it opens. Translated by Eknath Easwaran in *The Upanishads* (Petaluma, California: Nilgiri Press, 1987).

140 THE BRAHMIN This is the concluding chapter of the Dhammapada of the Compassionate Buddha (see entry for page 43 above). The word *brahmin* literally means "one who is worthy of knowing God" (Brahman). Translated by Eknath Easwaran in *The Dhammapada* (Petaluma, California: Nilgiri Press, 1985).

147 THE CITY OF BRAHMAN From the Chandogya Upanishad, 8:1.1–4.3 (see also notes for page 30 above). Translated by Eknath Easwaran in *The Upanishads* (Petaluma, California: Nilgiri Press, 1987).

150 THE ISLAND From the Sutta Nipata, 1093–94, one of the scriptures that traditionally preserve the Buddha's direct teachings. This translation is by Stephen Ruppenthal.

151 IN THE MIDST OF DARKNESS From an impromptu talk by Mahatma Gandhi addressed to the people of the United States in a radio broadcast from London in 1931. A more complete text may be found in *My Religion* (Ahmedabad, India: Navajivan, 1955).

152 WHAT IS REAL NEVER CEASES Bhagavad Gita, chapter 2, verses 13–30 (see note for page 36). This is the beginning of Lord Krishna's teachings before the epic battle at Kurukshetra, which Mahatma Gandhi said symbolizes the battle between right and wrong, good and evil, which takes place in the human heart. Translated for meditation by Eknath Easwaran.

155 THE LORD OF LIFE The Shvetashvatara Upanishad, canto 2 (see notes for page 129). Translated by Eknath Easwaran in *The Upanishads* (Petaluma, California: Nilgiri Press, 1987).

158　THE LORD IS MY SHEPHERD　Psalm 23 (King James Version) – a psalm of David, and surely one of the best-loved passages in the Jewish and Christian scriptures.

159　THE RULER WITHIN　The Katha Upanishad, part 2, canto 2 (see notes for page 52).

162　LET ME WALK IN BEAUTY　This prayer is thought to be Native American in origin and is sometimes attributed to the Sioux. This free rendering appeared in the *Friends Bulletin*.

165　FOUR THINGS THAT BRING MUCH INWARD PEACE　*The Imitation of Christ,* book 3, chapter 23 (see notes for page 46).

166　THE TREE OF ETERNITY　The Katha Upanishad, part 2, canto 3 (see notes for page 52).

169　EPISTLE ON LOVE　In his early days Saint Paul was Saul, a Jewish tent-maker in Tarsus soon after the time of Jesus, who persecuted the early Christians until he experienced a cataclysmic vision while traveling to Damascus. Later he said of this experience: "I am crucified with Christ: nevertheless I live; yet not I, but Christ liveth in me." He traveled and taught throughout Asia Minor and in Greece until his death in Rome, around A.D. 65.

170　THE WAY OF PEACE　Caterinetta Fieschi Adorna was born to a noble family in Genoa in 1447, and for many years after her marriage at sixteen she was caught between her spiritual yearnings and the demands of her marriage and her position in society. At twenty-seven she experienced a soul-shattering conversion, and from then on her life became a remarkable combination of intense devotion and practical service of the sick and destitute. Her husband was transformed by her example and joined her in her work. This translation is from G. Ripley, *Life and Doctrine of Saint Catherine of Genoa* (New York: Christian Press Association Publishing Co., 1896).

171　ENTERING INTO JOY　Saint Augustine was born in North Africa in 354 and lived into the last stages of collapse of the Roman Empire. His *Confessions,* one of the world's great pieces of autobiographical literature, tells the story of a brilliant, passionate young man who learned to channel all his passions toward God. This translation from book 9, chapter 10, is by Michael N. Nagler.

172 YOU ARE THAT From the Chandogya Upanishad, chapter 6. The refrain "You are That" (in Sanskrit, *Tat tvam asi*) is one of the "great utterances" that encapsulate the teachings of the Upanishads (see also notes for page 30). Translated by Eknath Easwaran in *The Upanishads* (Petaluma, California: Nilgiri Press, 1987).

174 LET NOTHING UPSET YOU This little poem of Saint Teresa of Avila, dear to Catholics around the world, was found in her breviary after her death. (See notes for page 39.)

175 PRAYER FOR PEACE Composed by Swami Omkar, the venerable head of Shanti Ashram in Andhra Pradesh and of the Peace Center on the Nilgiris, South India.

Acknowledgments

We are grateful to the following publishers for permission to reprint selections from their books:

Navajivan Trust for "The Path" (p. 115), and "In the Midst of Darkness" (p. 151), from M. K. Gandhi, *My Religion* (Ahmedabad: Navajivan, 1955)

Ramakrishna-Vivekananda Center for "Songs from Ramakrishna" (pp. 93 *ff*), *from The Gospel of Sri Ramakrishna*, by "M.", translated by Swami Nikhilananda (copyright 1942 by Swami Nikhilananda: Ramakrishna-Vivekananda Center of New York, 1942); and for the "last message" of Sri Sarada Devi (p.63), "The Whole World Is Your Own," from *Holy Mother* by Swami Nikhilananda (copyright 1962 by Swami Nikhilananda: Ramakrishna-Vivekananda Center of New York, 1962)

The Vedanta Society of Southern California for selections 3–6 of "Invocations to the Upanishads," from *The Upanishads: Breath of the Eternal,* translated by Swami Prabhavananda and Frederick Manchester (Hollywood: Vedanta Press, 1968); and for "May We Be United in Heart" (p.40) and "Hymn to the Divine Mother" (p.35), from *Prayers and Meditations Compiled from the Scriptures of India,* edited by Swami Prabhavananda and Clive Johnson (Hollywood: Vedanta Press, 1967)

The Paulist Press for "Radiant Is the World Soul" (p. 121), from *Abraham Isaac Kook,* translated by Ben Zion Bokser (New York: Paulist Press, 1978), and for "Teach Me" (p. 106), from *The Fire and the Cloud: An Anthology of Catholic Spirituality,* edited by the Rev. David A. Fleming, S.M. (New York: Paulist Press, 1978)

Penguin Books Ltd. for "Only God I Saw" (p. 51), from Reynold A. Nicholson, *The Mystics of Islam* (Arkana, 1989; copyright Reynold A. Nicholson, 1914)

Other sources and translators are mentioned in the Notes.

Index by Tradition

Hinduism

Judaism

Native American

Taoism

Index of Titles & First Lines

Library of Congress Cataloging-in-Publication Data:

Easwaran, Eknath.
God makes the rivers to flow : selections from the sacred
literature of the world / chosen for daily meditation by
Eknath Easwaran – 2nd ed.
p.   cm.
Includes bibliographic references and indexes.
ISBN 0–915132–69–9 (alk. paper) : $22.00.
ISBN 0–915132–68–0 (pbk. : alk. paper) : $12.95
1. Meditations.   2. Religious literature.   I. Title.
BL624.2.E37 1991
291.4'3—dc20   91–33664
CIP